John W. Phelps

Madagascar

John W. Phelps

Madagascar

ISBN/EAN: 9783337317690

Printed in Europe, USA, Canada, Australia, Japan

Cover: Foto ©Andreas Hilbeck / pixelio.de

More available books at **www.hansebooks.com**

THE ISLAND

OF

MADAGASCAR.

A SKETCH,

DESCRIPTIVE AND HISTORICAL.

BY

GEN. J. W. PHELPS,

MEMBER OF THE VERMONT HISTORICAL SOCIETY, ETC.

(Copyrighted 1883, by John B. Alden.)

NEW YORK.

JOHN B. ALDEN, PUBLISHER,

1883.

PREFACE.

Nothing is claimed for this sketch as an original production by the writer. It has been written with the view of extending reliable knowledge of African affairs among our American citizens, who, as their interests and welfare have become peculiarly involved with those of the African race, will have especial need of all information that may tend to enlighten them concerning the past history and future hopes of that race. The facts given have been drawn chiefly from accounts published by observers of excellent character, often in their own words, and will enable the reader to form a correct idea of the present relation in which the people of England and France stand towards those of Madagascar; and more particularly with respect to the efforts which have been made towards introducing Christian civilization into that island.

If these labors shall lead our American citizens who are charged with the affairs of a great and important government, to a more careful consideration of our moral obligations towards the true interests of Africa, and of the best manner of serving these interests through our Liberian colony, which lies on the opposite side of the African continent from Madagascar, the writer will consider himself amply rewarded. He has aimed at nothing more, and will regard himself happy if he shall have accomplished that.

MADAGASCAR.

CHAPTER I

Madagascar, the largest island in the world after Australia and Borneo, is separated from the African continent by the channel of Mozambique, which, at its narrowest point, is about two hundred miles wide. It lies almost wholly between the southern tropic and the equator, and has a length of nine hundred miles, running northeasterly, in a general parallel direction with the African coast. With an average breadth somewhat exceeding two hundred miles, it contains an area of more than two hundred thousand square miles, being nearly twice as large as Great Britain and Ireland, and five times as large as the State of New York.

The existence of this island was first made known to the European world by Marco Polo, who, in his travels in the East, which were performed in the thirteenth century, mentions it by the name of Magaster. The origin of this name is not known; nor do the inhabitants of the island recognize it as applied to their country, for which they have no distinct appellation. There are evidences that it has been visited by Moors, Arabs, and Hindostanee from very early times, but the first arrival of Europeans upon its shores dates from the year 1506, at which time it was discovered by Lawrence Almeida, son of the Portuguese Viceroy of India. The Portuguese soon established a settlement upon it, and built a fort, which however never flourished. Nor did the Dutch, who also found it a convenient stopping place on their way to the East, ever make much progress in the island.

The situation of the island seemed to render it a very desirable stopping place and depot for the European vessels that were beginning to enter upon the commerce of the East. It lies about eighteen hundred miles from the Cape of Good Hope, five hundred and fifty from Mauritius, and four hundred and fifty from the Isle of Bourbon.

The French made their first attempt to establish a settlement on the island in 1642. A patent was granted by Cardinal Richelieu, to Captain Rivault, for the exclusive right of sending ships and forces to Madagascar and the neighboring islands, to establish a plantation or colony for the promotion of commerce. Out of this charter grew the French East India Company, and their first ship was sent out in 1642 under Captain Coquet, who had already prepared to sail to the island on his own account for a cargo of ebony. This expedition, which was furnished with two governors and directed to take possession of the island in the King's name, first landed and took possession of the Isle of Bourbon and other small islands in the vicinity. It chose a point upon the Island of Madagascar which proved to be exceedingly unhealthy, for the low lands are subject to a most fatal fever; but it finally fixed upon a spot on the south side of the bay of Taocanara, and built a fort which they called Dauphin. This fort is 150 feet above the level of the sea, and commands the road; so that no enemy's ships could escape the fire of its batteries. The landing to it is rendered difficult by a steep declivity; it is of an oblong form, and enclosed with strong walls of lime and gravel well cemented. This point is in the southeastern portion of the island; the anchorage in the roadstead is excellent, and the harbor is screened by the Isle of St. Clair from the heavy sea gales, so that the entrance is convenient at all times for large ships.

Though the French colony has never flourished to any considerable extent, yet as it furnished slaves and other supplies for the Mauritius and Isle of Bourbon, it has been resorted to by the French with varying conditions and some few intermissions down to the present day. It at one time contained a Catholic bishop, three missionaries and two lay brethren, with a chapel, monastery, and library. Efforts were made by these missionaries as early as 1647 to construct a grammar of the native language, and vocabularies were formed, together with a catechism for the use of young converts, copies of which are still extant, interlined with French and Latin. But it does not appear that letters or the Christian religion ever made much progress in the island until the arrival of a party of English missionaries in 1818. At no time has any system of European colonization prospered there.

The attention of the English was called to the Island of

Madagascar soon after its discovery. It is stated by Flacourt that in 1642 the English had an establishment at St. Augustine's Bay, consisting of 200 men. During the troublesome times of Charles the First, the English turned an unquiet gaze to some foreign object to divert their minds from the distractions at home, and considerable interest was excited in the public by a report given of this island by an embassy from England to the King of Persia. A Mr. Richard Boothby, merchant of London, who had dwelt upon the island for three months, gave the following account of it: "It is my humble opinion, very possible, that whatsoever prince of christendom is once really possessed of, and strongly settled in that brave, fruitful and pleasant island, by computation three times as big as England, may with ease be emperor and sole monarch of the East Indies, with all the multitude of its large and rich kingdoms; which, no doubt, but the eyes of many European princes are fixed upon, but that great disturbances in most parts thereof, as at present unhappily in England, hinder and give impediments to their wished designs, which, in zeal to God's glory, my gracious sovereign's honor, and my native country's welfare and prosperity, I from the bottom of my heart wish that some more learned and persuasive pen than mine, rude and ignorant, might prevail with his gracious Majesty, King Charles, the right honorable High Court of Parliament, and all true-hearted able persons of the nobility, gentry, etc., to take in hand, even in these obstructive times, to adventure each man some small proportion of means throughout this kingdom, which, though but small to every particular person, yet, undoubtedly, would amount to a very considerable sum of money, sufficient to undertake that action as a business of State. That I may give the best advice and encouragement in this affair, that my weak capacity will allow, I shall descend to the following particulars."

The writer then goes into a lengthy detail of the beauties and advantages of this "second land of Canaan, or paradise of the world."

"It is a great pity," says he, "that so pleasant and plentiful a country should not be inhabited by civilized people, or rather Christians; and that so brave a nation, as to person and countenance, only black or tawny, should be so blindly led in their devotions, being, as some suppose, Mahometans, in regard to their manner and custom of circumcision; or rather, as some suppose, descended from Abraham. A happy thing it were, both for them and this kingdom, if that project had, or should go forward, which a gentleman in Huntingdonshire, bred a merchant, in love told me, which he heard from others, or rather, as I understood it, from Bishop Moreton's own mouth, that if the bishops of England, lately dismissed from voting in Parliament, and tyrannizing in temporal authority, should still continue in disrespect with the King and Parliament, they, or most part of them, would go and plant a colony in Madagascar, and endeavor to reduce those ignorant souls to Christianity. God grant that, by them or others, such a pious design my speedily take effect."

The numerous advantages possessed by the island made such a strong appeal to the public mind that it was agreed at the council-board, says Mr. Boothby, that Prince Rupert should go as Viceroy to Madagascar. He was to have twelve sail from King Charles, and thirty merchantmen to attend him to the plantation, and to have supplies yearly sent out from England. It was likewise agreed upon, and a charge given to the governor, Sir Maurice Abbot, Sir Henry Garway, and others of the committee of the Honorable East India Company, to give all their loving assistance and furtherance to Prince Rupert in this design, whensoever he came into Asia or India, and all other parts adjacent to the Island of Madagascar.

Mr. Boothby was present "when this was ordered at the council-table, and the charge given to the aforesaid governor and committee of the East India Company; but Prince Rupert going into France and Germany about his weighty affairs, in the meantime it was thought fit, and concluded upon, that the Earl of Arundel, earl marshal of England, should go governor for Madagascar, it being the most famous place in the world for a magazine. This honorable earl was in such resolution and readiness that there were printed bills put up on the pillars of the Royal Exchange, and in other parts of the city, that abundantly showed his forwardness in promoting a plantation in Madagascar; but a new Parliament being called, it put a stop to the design of Madagascar."

The next account of the island which we have in connection with the English is given in the history of Robert Drury, who from the year 1702 until 1717 was detained there by the natives as a slave. Drury had received but a limited education, and at an early period of life was induced, as many other youths have been, through love of adventure and romance, to seek his fortune at sea. At the age of fourteen he embarked as passenger on board a ship bound for the East Indies, and sailed from London in 1701. He was destined to learn that, according to his own account, *wilful persons never want woe;* for on his return from Bengal, the ship, the De Grave, was shipwrecked on the coast of Madagascar. A large part of the crew escaped, and reached the shore near the southernmost point of the island; but they afterwards became scattered, and little is known of their subsequent history. Drury became a domestic slave, and as such passed from the hands of one proprietor to another, experiencing every variety of treatment, which reminded him with bitter regrets of his reckless desertion of his own pleasant home. The first impressions made upon his mind after reaching the shore are given in the following extracts:

"The country began now to be alarmed, and we had already two or three hundred negroes flocking round us, picking up several pieces of silk and fine calicoes; the muslin they had little regard for. Our goods were driven ashore in whole bales; for, what with saltpeter and other things, we reckoned there might be three hundred tons left, after all that was thrown overboard at sundry times before.

"One of the negroes brought an ox to us, and intimated by sundry signs that we should kill him; but we made signs to them again to shoot him for us, we having no ammunition; when one of them perceived this, he lent us his gun, ready charged, and with it one of our men shot the bullock on the spot.

"It was extremely shocking to see the negroes cut the beast, skin and flesh together, and sometimes the entrails also, then toss them into the fire or ashes, as it happened, and eat them half roasted. I shuddered for fear they should devour us in like manner; for they seemed to me to be a kind of Cannibals, of whom I had heard very dreadful stories. Everything, in short, appeared horrible to nature, and excited in us the most dismal apprehensions."

The melancholy fate of that portion of the ship's crew with which Drury was associated more than confirmed his worst fears. The chief who ruled over that part of the island where they were wrecked, having most probably some supposed or real injury to revenge upon the white people, had them all bound and brought before him, when they were all butchered in the most barbarous manner; Drury alone being permitted to live, for the purpose of attending upon the grand-son of the chief in the capacity of a slave.

It was a custom in certain parts of the island that the

slaughtering of cattle, deemed a highly honorable avocation, was appropriated by the nobility; and as Drury was supposed to be a son of the captain of the ship, and therefore a person of rank, he was treated better than the ordinary run of slaves, and was appointed to the office of honor and profit of slaughtering cattle.   By this means he obtained a more regular supply of provisions than he could have otherwise received from his various masters.   His duties, in times of peace, consisted chiefly in tending his master's cattle, and driving them to water, for which they were frequently sent a distance of six or seven miles.   Digging wild yams and managing bees and honey were other occupations in which he was employed. Whether from these qualifications, or from the prevalent ideas, not only that he was a person of rank, but that white people ought never to be held in bondage, Drury enjoyed many advantages as a slave, and was so highly esteemed that the possession of his services was often the subject of envy amongst the chieftains of that part of the country.   His constant endeavor, however, was to find some means of getting away to the sea shore, where he hoped to find some vessel in which he might make his escape.   At times the rigors of his lot were rendered more tolerable by this hope brightening almost into a certainty, as he listened to those who spoke of the different sea-ports accessible from the neighborhood in which he was detained; but often before he could reach one of these ports, the results of war plunged him into the deepest despair, by placing him in the power of a more vigilant master, or removing him, along with the chieftain he served, to some district more remote from the sea.

Encouraged by the prospect of reaching St. Augustine's Bay, he made more than one bold adventurous attempt to escape from his masters.   On one occasion, after pursuing his lonely course for many days, attended with almost incredible hardships, just as the hope of final success was gaining advantage over the fear of detection, he came to the banks of a river, so wide and deep as to present an almost impassable barrier to his progress.

" As I was searching," he says, " for a proper place to wade through, or swim over, I spied a large alligator.   I still walked upon the banks, and in a short time saw three more.   This was a mortifying stroke, and almost dispirited me.   I went on until I came to a shallower place, where I entered the river about ten yards; but seeing an alligator make towards me, I ran directly back. He pursued me until I got into very shallow water, and then he turned back into the deep, for they will never attack a man near the shore. It nettled me to be stopped by a river that was scarcely a hundred yards over. At length I recollected that in the neighborhood of Bengal, where there are the largest alligators in the world, fires are often made at the head and stern of the boat, so that they pass the rivers in safety. Distress puts a man's invention upon the rack; something like this, thought I, must be done; for it was to no purpose to stay there, neither could I go back. So making choice of a stick for a fire-brand, I cut it into long splinters, and waited till it grew dark; then, after I had bound my two fire-sticks to the top of one of my lances, I went into the water, and, recommending myself to the care of Providence, turned upon my back and swam over, with my two lances and hatchet in one hand, and my fire-brand burning in the other, my lamba being twisted and tied fast about my loins."

At last the welcome sight of St. Augustine's Bay, with its road, where ships were wont to touch, presented itself to the weary and solitary traveler as he stood on the summit of a hill of considerable elevation. It does not appear, however, that any means of escape from the country were available at that time; for he was obliged to place himself under the protection of a chieftain who had formerly shown him kindness, and who required his service in the wars in which he was then engaged.

It is worthy of remark, that although the pirates are considered to be the originators of the slave-trade in Madagascar, yet more than one account occurs in Drury's narrative where the barter of men for foreign goods is spoken of as the customary trade of the country, even at that time. Drury was informed by a person who had lived considerable time in the country, that to a place called Masseelege (probably the Methelege of the pirates) to the northward, there came, once a year, a Moorish ship, that brought silk lambas and many other things to trade for slaves. And again, towards the conclusion of the term of his captivity, he speaks of two ships staying at Youngoule, where slaves were sent to be sold in exchange for fire-arms and other goods. It seems probable, however, that these were but occasional visits, made chiefly by marauding vessels, and that it was not until after the vessels of the pirates had been destroyed, that this commerce in human beings became a regular and organized system of barbarous traffic in the island.

Whilst Drury was residing at a sea-port on the western coast, called Youngoule, an English ship, the Clapham Galley, Captain Wilks, commander, arrived there to take in a cargo of slaves; and a number were accordingly taken down to the coast to be sold. The master whom Drury served at that time was collecting slaves for this purpose; and he, delighted with the idea of thus escaping from the country, engaged a friend to intercede with his master and mistress that he might be sold with the rest; but being a prisoner of war, and probably too highly prized for his services, he was denied the privilege of being sold with the native slaves.

Before the ship set sail, however, Drury (to use his own words) "endeavored to inform the captain by this stratagem: I took a leaf, which was about two inches broad and a foot and a half long, and marked upon it these words: 'Robert Drury, son of Mr. Drury, living at the King's Head in Old Jewry, now a slave in the Island of Madagascar, in the country of Youngoule.' I desired the favor of one who was going to the sea-side, to deliver this leaf to the first white man he saw; and when he returned, I asked him what answer he had brought. 'None at all,' replied he; 'for I suppose the white man did not like it, since he threw the leaf away, though I am sure it was as good, if not better, than that which you gave me: it is true I *dropped yours*, but then I pulled one of the best I could find off a tree.'" "My heart," says Drury, "was ready to break at this disappointment; whereupon I turned from him, and went directly into the woods to give vent to my tears."

Some years after this bitter disappointment, Drury obtained his long wished-for liberation; and the circumstances of this event are best described in his own words. Aware that two ships were then waiting for slaves at Youngoule, every intelligence respecting them obtained an interest in his mind, such as none but a captive could have experienced; and he feelingly relates the circumstance of his final escape from slavery in the following words:—

"I was sitting with my master one evening, when two men came in with a basket of palmetto leaves sewed up, and delivered it to the chief, who opened it, and finding a letter, asked the men what they meant by giving him that? 'The captain,' they said, 'gave it us for your white man, but we thought proper to let you see it first.' 'Pray,' said the chief, 'give it all to him. Here, Robin, your countrymen have sent you a present; what it is I do not know, but to me it appears of very little value.' Accordingly I took the basket; and with the letter there were pens, ink, and paper, in order to my returning an answer. The superscription was this: ' *To Robert Drury, in the Island of Madagascar.*'

" I was so astonished, that at first I had no power to open it, concluding I was in a dream; but at length recovering from my surprise, after a little recollection I opened it, and found it came from Captain William Macket; the contents were to the effect following:

" That he had a letter on board from my father, with full instructions, as well from him as the owners of the vessel, to purchase my liberty, let it cost what it would; and, in case I could not possibly come down myself, to send him word the reason of it, and what measures he should take to serve me."

The chief was astonished to see the change in Drury's countenance as he read the letter; and when informed of the intelligence it conveyed, his surprise appeared unbounded; and, as he examined the paper, he said that he had heard before of such a method of conveying information, but was wholly at loss to conceive how it could be done without witchcraft: a feeling exactly coinciding with the impression made on the minds of the Society and Sandwich Islanders, when they first witnessed the transmission of intelligence by means of writing.

It was not without considerable persuasion and many entreaties, that the chieftain and his family could be induced to part with the English slave; but it was at last agreed upon that he should be permitted to go with the captain, on the condition that the latter would provide the chief with a good gun, which he promised to call Robin, in remembrance of his slave.

The joy experienced by Drury on his happy liberation exceeded all bounds; though the novelty of his feelings, after fifteen years' captivity among a barbarous people, rendered his situation almost too strange and exciting for enjoyment. He returned to England with Captain Macket, and on the 9th of September, 1717, again reached the shores of his native country, after an absence of sixteen years. It is stated by Drury, in his own account of this joyful event, that, after landing, he could not set forward on his journey to London without returning God thanks, in the most solemn manner, for his safe arrival, and for his deliverance from the many dangers he had escaped, and the miseries he had so long endured.

After the expression of such feelings, and especially after perusing the history of his protracted sufferings, it is equally melancholy and astonishing to see Robert Drury (the most unlikely of all men to be engaged in the same cruel system of oppression by which he had himself been held in such degrading bondage) embarking, in less than two years after his return to England, as a slave dealer for Madagascar, and, by his own testimony, using all his knowledge of the country in directing captains and others to the places where the unhappy captives, whom he was dooming to a harder lot than he had suffered, were likely to be obtained in the greatest numbers ! He appears to have made extensive purchases of slaves; and, after a residence of more than a year in the island, proceeded to Virginia in North America, and there disposed of his miserable cargo.

The conduct of the pirates, in promoting a war for the purpose of obtaining slaves, which was so long the most terrible scourge of Madagascar, has been universally stamped with infamy, and their proceedings in encouraging this inhuman traffic are justly and naturally associated with all that is reprobate in character and fiendish in cruelty, and it might seem congenial employment to pirates—to men accustomed to kill and destroy all who held the property which they coveted; but the conduct of Drury, who in many respects may be regarded as an honest-hearted Englishman, and who had been taught by sufferings himself to see the beauty of respecting the rights of others, gives us another evidence, and of the most impressive kind, of that false opinion and depraved feeling to which all become liable who are brought under the nefarious influences of slavery.

With respect to the connection of pirates with Madagascar and the slave trade, a detailed account is neither practicable nor necessary. We learn, however, that from the moment that the commerce of the Western world became active in the Eastern seas, from that moment European pirates began to make their appearance there. And for the same reason that European powers desired a foothold in the island for the better carrying on their intercourse with the oriental nations, the pirates found it a convenient depot for striking at European commerce. It seemed to offer the same advantages in this respect for the Indian Ocean that the Barbary States did for the Mediterranean Sea.

Among the more notable pirates who visited the coast of Madagascar was Captain William Kid, who in the reign of

William III had received a commission from that monarch, to go out in charge of a ship, with "full power and authority to apprehend, seize, and take into custody all pirates, freebooters, and sea-rovers, which he should meet upon the seas, or upon the coast of any country.' With this commission Captain Kid sailed in the Adventure, galley of thirty guns with eighty men, and directed his course to Madagascar, the great resort of such marauders as he was in search of. For some time he cruised about in the neighborhood of the island, but the pirate-ships being most of them out in search of prey, his provisions and resources began to diminish, while his hopes of success became increasingly faint. While he continued in this state, he began to think of abandoning the object for which he had been sent out, and finally made known to his crew the design he had conceived of becoming himself a pirate. The scheme was but too readily adopted by his comrades, who, under the command of their unprincipled leader, commenced a course of lawless cruelty and bloodshed, which terminated in the apprehension, trial, and execution of their traitorous leader.

Another leading pirate was a Frenchman by the name of Misson, who, together with his comrade Caraccioli, established a sort of republican commonwealth, upon the northeastern coast. Here they were afterwards joined by Captain Tew, and being all men of superior education and abilities to those generally engaged in the profession of piracy, the affairs of their settlement were for some time conducted with no inconsiderable degree of political skill, which was attended with a measure of success. They built a fort and town, cultivated the land, and had a Senate house in which they made wise laws for the infant colony. From this colony, which they called Libertatia, they sent forth their ships on marauding expeditions, and were so successful as to add greatly to their wealth and power. It was an infant Rome, of a marine stamp, plundering the treasures of other people to add to its own. They made friends with the natives, who through intercourse and barter shared in the plunder, and thus found it to their interest to assist in building and navigating vessels for increasing it. On one occasion they captured a Moorish vessel, bound for Mecca with pilgrims; and there being on board one hundred women, who were accompanying their friends and parents on their pilgrimage, the pirates detained these as wives for the people of their colony, with a view to its greater stability, and the contentment of the men under their command.

. The pirates continued their depredations with success until the year 1721, when the nations of Europe, alarmed at the enormous losses sustained by their commerce, finally united to clear the Indian Ocean from these depredators. The capture of two Portuguese vessels of war by the pirates on the same day, on board of one of which were the Count Receisa and the Archbishop of Goa, aroused the attention of Europe to the formidable proportions which the power of the pirates had assumed.

Elated with their past successes the pirates made a long resistance. Considerable squadrons were required to oppose them, and the most rigorous and exemplary punishments were inflicted upon them. Their vessels were pursued to the most secret recesses of the coast and there destroyed by fire.

The loss of their ships deprived the pirates of the means of interrupting the commerce between India and Europe, and confined them to their settlements on the coast of Madagascar. Forced to give up their wandering and predatory life, they plunged into a different kind of villainy, which has left upon their memory a deeper stain. The source of wealth which they had lost in being shut out from the plunder of richly freighted ships, they might compensate for by a sale of the natives as slaves. And in the pursuit of this plan, they were favored and protected by European powers, since it was a common source of enrichment to all.

As a means of procuring slaves the pirates stimulated their former friends the natives to frequent wars, and for the captives which either party made they gave in exchange firearms and ammunition, which, while being much coveted by the natives, served to incite to further wars and bloodshed among them. And in this respect we can hardly see any difference between the wars thus got up and the recent war of rebellion among us, since that war originated in the avowed purpose of maintaining the system of slavery which these Madagascar pirates were thus laboring to build up.

Before that period, the trifling divisions among the natives, arising from their peculiar social yet barbarous habits, never lasted long, nor left traces of deadly animosity behind them; but by this double system of treachery and bloodshed, the whole country was involved in all the miseries of violently agitated and ferocious passions, which have since diffused over the entire population every species of suffering, outrage and crime. The pirates did more than merely instigate the islanders to these internecine wars. Numerous instances are related, in which they actually engaged themselves in the treacherous and sanguinary wars of the natives. On one occasion two ships took in a cargo of six hundred slaves, as the reward of their assistance in a military expedition against some towns which a chief of the district wished to subdue.

Some of the persistent efforts of the French to colonize the island are not without interest. In 1767 the French Minister, the Duke de Praslin, presented a plan for the establishment of a colony at Fort Dauphin, which received the royal approbation. This plan was founded on the conviction that a purely military establishment was unsuitable; and that it was only by conciliatory means that the confidence and attachment of the natives was to be gained. It laid down as leading ideas that—"There was no necessity for sending troops and squadrons for conquest, nor for transporting a whole society at great expense: better arms and better means will promote the establishment, without expending much money. It is only by the force of example, morals, religion, and a superior policy, that we propose to subdue Madagascar. The society there is already formed; and nothing is necessary but to invite it to us, and to direct it according to our views, which will meet with no obstacles, as they will interest the Malagasy themselves, by the advantage of a reciprocal exchange."

Monsieur Maudave, who was sent out to establish this colony, reached the island in 1768, took formal possession of the government of Fort Dauphin, and made immediate preparations for the execution of the plan. It was not long, however, before this equitable and benevolent project was entirely relinquished, on the plea of having discovered that the establishment was founded on impracticable principles. It was doubtless found to be very difficult to make a barbarous people the chief means of their own civilization and refinement, without first converting them to the Christian religion.

The next effort made by the French at the colonization of Madagascar was through the agency of an extraordinary character by the name of Count Benyowsky, a Polish nobleman. This person was distinguished by an adventurous career and a life of romantic incident which bordered on the marvelous. In early life he had taken an active part in the political affairs of his own country; and falling under the displeasure of the Russian government, was banished to Siberia, whence he speedily effected his escape, by engaging a number of his fellow-sufferers in a conspiracy of so daring and extensive a

nature that they finally left Kamtschatka in possession of two
ships, and at the head of more than a hundred men, of whom
he was elected commander.

After enduring all the strange vicissitudes incident to a
voyage commenced under circumstances so unusual, and
touching at several places, Benyowsky at last sold his ships at
Canton, and, embarking himself and his crew on board two
French trading vessels, arrived at the Isle of France in the
year 1772. From there he set sail for France, with the view
of receiving a commission to colonize the Island of Madagascar. This, after much trouble, he finally accomplished, and
returning, he landed with a small expedition at the Bay of
Autougil, in the island, on the 4th of February, 1774.

The Count was favorably received by the chiefs, and it
would appear that he was animated with the most benevolent
designs in their behalf. Among other measures he succeeded
in gaining their assent to the abolition of an old custom of
infanticide which prevailed in the island. But though opposed
to the slave-trade, there are instances where he yielded to its
baneful seductions himself. He drew up and designed for the
inhabitants of the island a very liberal form of government,
and succeeded in having himself solemnly recognized by three
of their kings sovereign of the whole country. Soon after
this event he again set sail for France, in order to form a treaty
of commerce and friendship with the king, and to obtain
thence proper persons to instruct the natives in the various
arts of civil life. On his arrival in France he had a long and
violent altercation with the government; at the close of which,
however, he so far gained his point, as to obtain swords for his
conduct during his command of Madagascar. While in France
his cause was ably advocated by Dr. Franklin; but as the
French Minister would have no further transactions with him,
he entered the service of the Emperor of Germany, to whom
he made proposals respecting his scheme of colonization. Not
meeting with success, he left the service of the Emperor and
went to London, where he drew up a declaration with proposals to his Britannic Majesty, offering "in the name of an
amiable and worthy nation, to acknowledge him lord para-
mount of Madagascar; the interior government, and all the
regulations of civilization, police, cultivation, and commerce
remaining independent; the chiefs and people being only vas-
sals to his Majesty."

Meeting with no encouragement from the British Ministry,

the Count set sail for America in the Robert and Ann, with a cargo suitable for the Madagascar market. He reached Baltimore in July, 1784, obtained another vessel and cargo, and sailed for Madagascar in the following October. On the 7th of July, 1785, he again cast anchor in Autougil Bay. He renewed his former friendship with the chiefs; seized a storehouse belonging to the French, and commenced building a town, intending to establish a factory there. Whilst thus engaged he was attacked by an expedition from the Isle of France, and fell mortally wounded while defending a fort against an assault.

It was in 1776 that Benyowsky abandoned the French settlement which he had formed in Madagascar, and for some years afterwards the French government appear to have given up all idea of establishing a colony in that island, confining their efforts to the maintenance of military posts and factories, for the purpose of trade with the natives, to obtain supplies of rice and bullocks for the Isle of France. It was made an auxiliary to the Isle of France as an important depot for those engaged in the slave-trade, which continued to be carried on to a great extent throughout the whole island, notwithstanding the declarations of the French Minister, that he considered the tendency of the traffic to be prejudicial to the Isle of France.

The French revolution, which took place soon after Benyowsky had abandoned the colony, so fully engaged the attention of the French government, that, amidst the tragical and appalling events which crowd the page of history, it was scarcely possible to entertain any new project relating to the occupation of a distant island. St. Domingo was a scene to which much of the public attention of France was at that time directed, and its subsequent separation from that country was an alarming indication of the power which such colonies possess, when they have acquired a practical knowledge of their own physical strength and resources.

In the year 1792, the French National Assembly deputed Mons. Lescallier to visit Madagascar, in order to ascertain whether it would be practicable to establish a colony once more in the island. In a report rendered by him he said that "Europeans have hardly ever visited this island but to ill treat the natives, and to exact forced services from them; to excite and foment quarrels amongst them, for the purpose of purchasing the slaves that are taken on both sides in the consequent wars: in a word, they have left no other marks of having been there, but the effects of their cupidity. The French government has, at long intervals, formed, or rather attempted to form, establishments amongst these people; but the agents in these enterprises have attended exclusively to the interests and emoluments of the Europeans, and particularly to their own profits; while the interests and well-being of the natives have been entirely forgotten: some of these ministerial delegates have even been dishonest adventurers, and have committed a thousand atrocities. It cannot, therefore, excite surprise, that sometimes they have experienced marks of the resentment of the Malagasy, who, notwithstanding, are naturally the most easy and sociable people on earth."

After the visit of Lescallier, no other attempt was made by the French to establish a settlement in the island; the wars which succeeded the revolution giving full employment to the national resources; so much so, that it was at one period in contemplation to extend the conscription law to the Isle of France, for the purpose of supplying the army at home; and during the short peace of 1801, Borg de St. Vincent was sent on an errand of this kind to Madagascar. The island, he said, "is capable of being made the first colony in the world, and would supply the loss of St. Domingo, if the French government chose. It possesses advantages far superior in many respects to that unhappy country. It would form a fine military position in any war that might ensue in the Indies. Its productions are infinitely more various, labor would be cheaper, its extent is more considerable, and it would afford a good retreat to those Americans, who, having lost everything by the revolution, are now dependent on our government, who might distribute lands amongst them, with the means of conveyance, and temporary existence there."

The French government had often been interrupted, as will have been seen by the perusal of these pages, in its plans for colonizing Madagascar. After the lull in the revolutionary tempest of 1801, the war broke out in Europe with greater violence than ever, and notwithstanding her successes at home, France saw her colonies fall, one after another, into the hands of her persevering rival. It was, however, a long time before Great Britain could effect the reduction of the Isles of France and Bourbon. Engaged in extensive enterprises in the European seas, her fleets were fully employed, and the squadron sent against those distant islands was too weak to effect the purpose. Great bravery was displayed in the engagements between opposing squadrons, and a landing was at length effected by the English on the Isle of France; but an unfavorable circumstance having occasioned the destruction of some of the British ships, the troops on shore were thus cut off from all hope of relief, and were compelled to surrender. The French therefore remained triumphant in those seas some years longer; and in 1807, an attempt was made to form a settlement at Foule Point in Madagascar by some Frenchmen from the Isle of France; but unfortunately having chosen the sickly season for the expedition, they were carried off almost to a man, by the fever incident to that part of the island.

But the continual interruptions which the British East India trade experienced from the French cruisers, rendered it absolutely necessary for the English to effect the reduction of the French strong-hold in the Isle of France. The French continued their annoyance from this favored island long after their power in India was extinct. It was calculated that the value of the prizes carried into the Isle of France during ten years, amounted to over 12,000,000 of dollars. The vessels thus taken were emptied of their cargoes, and sold to the Arabs, by whom they were afterwards taken again to Calcutta and sold.

It was not until the year 1810, that a competent expedition was fitted out, and dispatched by the English government against the Isle of France. On its arrival, the resistance it met with was comparatively feeble, and, after a short contest, the governor offered to capitulate, and finally surrendered the place. There were at that period in the harbor, six frigates, three Indiamen, and twenty-four large merchant vessels, all of which fell of course into the hands of the victors. Soon after this, the Isle of Bourbon was also taken possession of by the British; and immediately upon the conquest of these islands, the English sent a detachment to Foule Point, and another to Tamatave, to take possession of the forts formerly occupied by the French in Madagascar.

When the peace of 1814 was arranged, the Isle of Bourbon, which had changed its name to Reunion, was by treaty ceded to the French; but the Isle of France, or Mauritius, as it is more generally called, a name given to it by the Dutch when the island was in their possession, remained in the possession of the English, to whom it still belongs.

Soon after this period, a proclamation was issued by the governor of the Mauritius (Sir Robert Farquhar) taking possession of Madagascar in the name of the King of Great Britain;

but this act was loudly protested against by the French governor of Bourbon. It is probable that amongst other reasons for objections to this measure, the French governor was influenced by the fact, that the Isle of Bourbon, as well as the Mauritius, was deeply involved in the slave-trade, which the British government had recently renounced, and to which governor Farquhar was avowedly and openly opposed. The abolition of the slave-trade by the British, in 1807, during the prevalence of the French revolutionary war, may in fact be regarded as a strong distinctive difference in favor of liberty in the struggle between the English and French, and which had no small effect in the direction given to the successes of the war.

The efforts of Governor Farquhar to introduce civilization and Christianity into Madagascar, and to suppress the slave-trade there, aided by the London Missionary Society, and thwarted mischievously by fellow officers of his own government, much to the injury and discredit of the national service —would furnish an interesting history of themselves. We shall give a succinct account of them; but before doing so, and to their clearer understanding, the reader will desire to form some idea of the island, its productions and inhabitants.

CHAPTER II.

In a geological point of view the island exhibits primitive formations, chiefly granite, sienite, and blocks of exceedingly pure quartz. Of this latter mineral, the natives make use to ornament the summits of their tombs. Grey-wacke, schist, clay slate, suitable for roofing, chalcedony, lime-stone, including various kinds of marble, basalt, sand-stone, are common in the island. Finely crystalized schools frequently occur, and in the lime-stone of apparently fresh water formation are found imbedded fossils, including serpents, lizards, chameleons, and several kinds of vegetables.

No subterranean fires are known to be at present in active, visible operation, yet indications of volcanic action frequently occur, and are strongly marked. Many of the rocks, for several miles together, are composed of homogeneous earthy lava; scoria and pumice are also occasionally discovered. Rock-salt, nitre, and pyrites yielding a valuable percentage of sulphur, are met with.

The country next the shore is generally flat and exceedingly low, in parts marshy and incapable of culture. The margin of level land along the sea-coast, consisting of rich meadow lands or rice grounds, extends on the eastern coast ten or fifteen miles inland; on the western side of the island it is from fifty to one hundred miles, and sometimes more, in width. In some parts of the eastern coast, the country becomes suddenly mountainous at the distance of about thirty miles from the sea. In the interior, beyond this margin of level ground, the country is diversified with hills of varied elevations, and extending in every direction. But in some parts of the island immense plains stretch, in comparatively cheerless solitude, over a wide extent of country, small spots here and there alone being under cultivation. Groves, with pleasing frequency, adorn the landscape; shrubs and brushwood decorate and clothe many parts of the island. The vast extent, the unbroken solitude and gloom of its impenetrable forests, where, under the continued influence of a tropical sun and a humid atmosphere, the growth and decay of vegetation, in its most uncontrolled spontaneity, has proceeded without interruption for centuries, present scenes of extensive and gigantic vegetation, in sublime and varied forms, rarely, perhaps, surpassed in any part of the world. Immense forests traverse the island in all directions, within which may be expected and realized all that is imposing, and wonderful, and venerable in the vegetable kingdom, where, for thousands of years no ax has been laid to their giant trunks, nor even have the footsteps of man ever broken the deep and impressive silence. It is with exceeding difficulty that their dark masses can be penetrated, owing partly to the insalubrity of the deep recesses, where the air itself can hardly circulate, and partly to the very situation of the forests themselves, stretching up the sides of precipitous mountains, spreading over hills broken by sudden and deep chasms, or tenaciously occupying an under soil, from whence the upper has been washed away by heavy rains and torrents, leaving merely a net-work of roots and fibres, with fallen and decayed timber, to support the foot of the passenger.

The country is diversified with mountains, lakes and rivers. The mountains of Ankasatra attain the height of 8,000 to 12,000 feet. Their summits rise from a broad table land in the interior, which, like that of Mexico, is itself considerably elevated. The summits of Ankasatra are generally basalt in various stages of decomposition, many of them being hard and solid within, while the external surface is soft and earthy, and evidently losing a portion every year by the action of the atmosphere. Several of the smaller elevations are sugar-loaf in form, and in these granite predominates.

Lakes lie among the mountains as well as in the low lands along the sea-coast. Some of them are remarkable for their natural beauty, others are esteemed for their utility, and many of them are large, being often a hundred miles in length, though they are quite narrow, sometimes not more than a mile in breadth. Saririaka, the name of one of the lakes signifies "image of ocean." There is a highly bituminous lake which is five miles in width and sixty miles in length. On the eastern coast of the island a series of lakes extends for a distance of two hundred miles. Several of these are remarkably beautiful, being spotted with islets of various dimensions, some of them clothed with verdure, and others enlivened with the habitations of men.

The rivers of Madagascar are numerous, and many of them are of considerable width, the greater number flowing into the sea on the western coast. But they are all less favorable for the purposes of trade and commerce than from their magnitude a traveler might be led to expect. At their junction with the sea they are generally choked with sand, and their course is often obstructed with cascades, falls, and rapids, rendering navigation dangerous if not impracticable. The sublime, gloomy, and unbroken solitude of some parts of the mountain scenery of the island is enlivened by cataracts of varied size.

The climate is exceedingly diversified, both in the range of its temperature, and the degrees of its salubrity. The heat in the low lands and on the coast is often intense, but in the interior and elevated parts of the country it is mild, the thermometer seldom rising above 85°. In the different sections every variety of temperature may be met with, from the oppressive heat of the coast, to the cold of the loftly Ankasatra range, on the summits of which ice may often be found; or the elevated regions in the northern part of the island, where showers of sleet are frequently encountered.

The temperature of the principal province, Ankova, in which the capital is situated, is agreeable to the European, the greatest heat being about 85°, and the lowest 40°. Though it is often sultry in the middle portions of the day, yet the mornings and evenings are always pleasant. In the winter months, from May to October, when the ground is frequently covered with hoar frost, the thermometer sometimes does not rise above 44° for days together. At other seasons, the fluctuations in the heat of the atmosphere are extreme and sudden. Often in the morning the thermometer is at 40°, or even at 38°, and rises to 75° or 80° between two and three o'clock in the afternoon of the same day.

The effluvia arising from the lakes and swamps near the coast, is extremely prejudicial to health; and by incautious exposure to this, either early in the morning or late at evening, the fatal seeds of the Malagasy fever may be so deeply received into the human system as never to be eradicated. But in Ankova, which is some five or six thousand feet above the level of the sea, and in the interior, the fever does not exist, except in the state of a relapse from the disease contracted on the coast.

The rain, during its season, usually commences every day at from two to four or six o'clock in the afternoon and continues for a few hours, sometimes lasting through the night. It is generally accompanied with heavy thunder and much lightning. The trade winds prevail during the greater part of the year, and blow from the east or southeast; but the rains are often accompanied by high winds from the west, occasionally northwest, and not unfrequently from the southwest. The rain is occasionally mingled with hail; and showers of hail stones, at times as large as walnuts, have proved exceedingly injurious to vegetation. The *Rambondanitra*, "tail of heaven," that is, waterspout, and the *Tadio*, "twist," that is, whirlwind, are not uncommon, and often exceedingly destructive both to houses and plantations in the interior of the island. Houses are at times struck by lightning, and scarcely a year passes without several lives being lost from the same cause. Meteors are occasionally seen, and earthquakes are not unknown.

Among the numerously varied vegetable productions of the island we may mention the following:—The baobab, ebony, the *tapia edulis* on which a native silk worm is extensively reared, the tamarind, Indian fig, Indian betel, dragon tree, bamboo, the trees from which gum copal and gum elastic are derived, etc., etc. The island abounds in spices, in ginger, wild pepper, capsicums, tumeric, etc., and also in the sugar-cane, cotton-plant, tobacco, hemp, indigo-plant, and several kinds of dye-woods.

Among the articles of food may be mentioned, first, rice,

which is the principal edible of the natives, and of which there are eleven varieties. It is the general belief of the people that this plant is of comparatively recent introduction into the island, although it has been known there for several hundred years. So also with the cocoa-nut, which is supposed to have been washed ashore on the island by the waves some hundred and fifty years ago. The bread-fruit tree is of more recent introduction still. Plantains and bananas have been known from time immemorial. There are several kinds of yams, the manioc plant, Indian corn, large millet, beans, gourds, melons, pine apples and earth-nuts. Lemons, oranges, citrons, limes, peaches, and mulberries have long been introduced, and they flourish luxuriantly. Coffee has been found to succeed well. Wheat, barley, and oats have been produced, but are not much prized by the natives, and do not seem to flourish in their soil. The common potato is extensively cultivated and highly esteemed.

Honey and wax are abundant, and many kinds of oil, including that from the palma Christi, are obtained from the numerous vegetable productions of the country.

The ornithology of the island is but comparatively little known. Domestic poultry is abundant, and pheasants, partridges and guinea-fowl, both wild and tame, are common. Besides the birds which appear to be natives of the island, peacocks, turkeys, geese and ducks have been introduced. There are pigeons, turtle-doves, eagles, owls, kites, crows, hawks, paroquets with their gay plumage and querulous voices, etc., etc. Wild geese, ducks and other water-fowl abound in the lakes and rivers.

Although the quadrupeds of Madagascar extend to but few varieties, they comprehend the kinds most useful and essential to a nation in the early stages of its civilization. Horned cattle are numerous, both tame and wild. Many of the latter resemble in shape and size the cattle of Europe. The former are of the zebu, or buffalo kind, and have a large hump or bunch on the back between the shoulders. Herds of cattle constitute the principal wealth of a number of the chiefs or nobles, and not only furnish a considerable portion of their means of subsistence, but are exported in large numbers to the islands of Bourbon and Mauritius, and furnished to the shipping visiting the coast for supplies. Besides cattle, sheep, swine, and goats are also abundant. The sheep, which appear to be aboriginal, resemble those of the Cape of Good Hope, covered with short hair instead of wool, and having large tails weighing from ten to twenty pounds each.

Dogs and cats, both wild and tame, hedge-hogs, badgers, baboons, monkeys, foxes, squirrels, rats and mice abound in the island.

Among the amphibious animals the crocodile is the most conspicuous. As it is held in veneration by the inhabitants, its numbers are not diminished by the destructive agency of man, except in the use of its eggs, and in consequence the fresh waters of the island abound with it. In some parts, the natives affirm that they are so numerous as to cause the place to resemble a plain covered with bullocks. They shun brackish and salt water, and their favorite places are the deep, rugged banks of a river or lake overhung with trees, and containing numerous cavities in which they can hide themselves, having also a gradually sloping sandbank, up which they can crawl to deposit their eggs. They feed principally upon fish, and may be seen and heard chasing their prey in the waters of the lake with astonishing velocity, and apparently in concert with each other. Bullocks are often seized as they are swimming across the water, and sometimes successfully attacked while drinking. But besides preying upon the animals that venture within their reach, they seize and eat with great voracity their own young. They have the sagacity to watch at those places where the females deposit their eggs, for the appearance of the young, which, on bursting the shell, usually run directly to the water. There a close-formed file of old crocodiles lie in wait, ready with their terrific teeth to devour these young as soon as they reach their genial element.

Many of the crocodile's eggs are destroyed by birds, especially by vultures, and also by serpents, but many more by the natives, who take off the shell, boil them, and dry them in the sun; after which they are preserved for use or sale. A single family have been seen to have as many as five hundred eggs drying at one time.

The laws by which life preys upon life, both animal and vegetable, in a tropical island left wholly to itself without the influence of divine revelation, the rank-growing swamps, teeming amidst their own decay, the darkling superstitions of man by which human life is destroyed, the struggle of the germ of life everywhere against the principle of decay, present one of the most curious and interesting subjects for the consideration of Christian man.

We shall now proceed to give some account of the natives of

Madagascar, and of the efforts which have been made to Christianize them.

There cannot of course be any very accurate estimate formed of the number of inhabitants which occupy the island, but it is supposed that they amount to five millions. But this is evidently less than the island has contained at former and not remote periods of its history. The embankments spread over large tracts of country, now overgrown with grass or brushwood, show that these parts were once regularly cultivated rice fields; and the scattered ruins of villages, or whole ranges of villages, now totally deserted, mark, though imperfectly, to what extent the country has been depopulated.

The island is not inhabited by one single race, but by a number of distinct tribes, more or less numerous, evidently derived from more then one source; differing also in many respects from each other, and remaining, though nominally comprised in one political empire, distinct and peculiar nations. There are points, however, in which they bear a general resemblance to each other. They are all rather below the middle stature, which but few exceeded; and their countenances do not exhibit that prominence of features which distinguish the European and most of the Asiatic nations. The men are more elegantly formed than the women, in whom there is a greater tendency to corpulency than in the other sex. The beards of the men are but slight, and are plucked out in youth. Their hands are not so warm to the touch as those of the Europeans, and their blood by the thermometer is colder. But the distinction between them the most strongly marked is that of color; and this, though presenting slight variations in each tribe, separates the population of Madagascar into two great classes, and is by some supposed to allow of its being traced to only two sources—the one distinguished by a light, exquisitely formed person, fair complexion, and straight or curling hair; the other more robust, and dark colored, with woolly hair. In one or the other of these two classes, the several tribes inhabiting the island may be included. In fact, so far as color is any indication, there are but two distinct races in Madagascar, the olive and the black; and the people may be supposed to be derived from a mixture of these two, forming all kinds of varieties of which their complexion, hair, and features are capable. From the character of the language, it may be presumed that the population is composed partly of the Malay and partly of the African race. But how the mixture came about, whether by colonization from the Malayan peninsula, the darker race being aboriginal to the island, or else introduced by emigration from the African continent, or perhaps brought in as slaves by the Malay settlers, or by Arab traders, we are left solely to conjecture.

As a means of throwing some light upon this subject, the language of the people is the only one upon which we can at present rely. It belongs, beyond a doubt, to that class of languages frequently denominated Malayan, but to which the term Polynesian appears far more appropriate. The fact that there was a great similarity in all the languages spoken in the islands of the eastern seas had been remarked by Cook and other voyagers, and from the commercial and political ascendency formerly held by the Malays in those parts, the name "Malayan" was given to all which resembled that language. A more extensive acquaintance, however, with them, has led to the conclusion that these dialects are not to be regarded as descended from the Malay, but as sustaining the relation of sisterhood to it, and to each other.

The living Malay language now spoken, or the vernacular dialect in the Malayan peninsula, and other parts of the Eastern Archipelago, is itself only related to the great and comprehensive Polynesian language, just as that of New Zealand, Tahiti, or Madagascar, may be related to it. The two most remarkable circumstances, belonging to this Polynesian language are, the wide extent to which it has been carried and the tenacity with which it has retained its hold, even in the contiguity of other more copious and cultivated languages, spoken by immensely larger numbers, such as the Arabic, Hindoo, Chinese, and Indo-Chinese.

With regard to the extent of region over which it has traversed, and still prevails, it is scarcely needful to do more than to glance at the fact, that from Madagascar in the West, to Easter Island in the East, embracing more than half the circumference of the globe at the equator, and from the Sandwich Islands in the North, to the extremity of New Zealand in the South, being 4,000 miles of latitude, there is a manifest connection between many of the words by which the inhabitants of these islands express their simple perceptions, and in some instances of places the most remote from each other, a striking affinity; insomuch that we may pronounce the various dialects, in a collective sense, substantially one great language. One original language seems in a very remote period to have per-

vaded the whole Indian Archipelago, and to have spread
(perhaps with the population) towards Madagascar on one side,
and the islands of the South Sea on the other.

The origin of this one great language is veiled in an impenetrable obscurity; nor are there any satisfactory data on which
to build conclusions respecting the era when, or the circumstances under which, it obtained so wide a dissemination. An
attempt to ascertain which of the Polynesian dialects should
be considered as the parent stock, from whence the others
branched out, must prove as fruitless as would be that of de-
termining which of the Teutonic dialects gave birth to the
others. Some have been inclined to fix upon Java as the seat
of this Polynesian language, but its original seat, may, for
aught that is known to the contrary, have been buried, by some
great convulsion beneath the sea. If we reflect how few feet's
subsidence of the British Isles would entirely obliterate the
center of the English power and language, leaving no trace
save in the colonies that have sprung from that center, we can
see how easy it might have been for a similar event to have
occurred with the central source from which the people of
Madagascar may have derived their native tongue.

We give a comparison between a few Madagascar and Malay
words, so that the reader can judge himself of their resemblance and affinity:

Malagasy.	Malay.	English.
anaka,	anaka,	a child.
alona,	alun,	a wave.
ompa,	ompat,	calumny.
ova,	ubah,	change.
tahotra,	takout,	fear.
olitra,	ulat,	a worm.
voa,	buah,	fruit.
helatra,	kulut,	lightning.
taolana,	tulang,	bone.
hoditra,	kulit,	skin.
nosa,	nusy,	island.
lanitra,	langit,	sky.
tomotra,	tumit,	heel.
taona,	taun,	year.

There are many dialects spoken in the island, but that of the
province of Ankova, the country of the Hovas, may be regarded as the standard one. The inhabitants of this province are
industrious, ingenious, and comparatively wealthy. It is the

center of the empire, the seat of the government, and the scene of the principal efforts hitherto made in the country to introduce education, European improvements, arts and sciences, and to promote civilization. Its climate is the most healthy in the island. In the external characteristics, the greater part of Ankova may be considered hilly, rather than mountainous. Few of its eminences rise above five or six hundred feet above the general level of its surface. The capital itself, Tananarivo, is situated on the summit of a long, irregular hill, about five hundred feet in height. The summits in the neighborhood are distinguished as the scenes of legendary tales, recounting the mighty achievements of giants, and other monstrous beings, supposed to belong to a fabulous age. The altars built by former generations on the summits of these heights, to the memory of such extraordinary personages still exist, and are visited by the people as appropriate places for prayer and sacrifice to the manes of the mighty dead. On the tops of some of these hills are still existing the vestiges of ancient villages. Altars are also met with throughout the whole of Ankova, and frequently the sites chosen for them are high places and groves, such as we may suppose existed in Judea in the days of Solomon. The usual name for these altars is Vazimba, *i. e.*, altars raised to the Vazimba (Phoenicians)? the supposed aborigines of the central parts of the island. One of the most celebrated vestiges of antiquity is situated on the summit of the mountain Ambohimiangara. It is the ancient tomb of the renowned giant Rapeto. An altar is connected with the tomb, on which sacrifices are still offered.

The population of Ankova is widely scattered in numerous villages over the surface of the country, which usually contain from fifty to one hundred houses each. The capital, Tananarivo, was supposed to contain in 1836 about 20,000 inhabitants, but at the present time the population is probably somewhat larger. It is at the distance of some two hundred miles from Tamatave, the principal sea-port on the eastern coast of the island, between which two points the roads are kept designedly bad for the purpose of rendering the interior of the country difficult of access to Europeans. Most of the villages are situated on eminences, and are generally encircled, for security, by a deep fosse; the earth from which being thrown up on the inner side, forms a bank round the village, which renders it difficult to scale the sides of the ditch, and adds to the safety of the people. The Hovas ! 'ong to one of the tribes of straight hair and olive complexion. But there are some evidences that the dark colored tribes were the earliest settlers in the island, and may perhaps therefore be considered as the aborigines of the country, as tradition respecting the settlement of the fairer race invariably represents them as having, at the time of their arrival, found the country inhabited.

The peculiarities of the dark race are, a black complexion, and a taller stature than the olive colored tribes, stouter body, thick and projecting lips, curly or frizzly hair, a frank and honest bearing, or a grave or timid expression of countenance, exhibiting a full bust and resembling the Africans of the Mozambique shore.

The fairer race are distinguished by a light olive or copper skin, smaller stature, long hair, hazel or black eyes, erect figure, courteous and prepossessing address, active movements, with an open, vivacious aspect.

Although the intellectual capacities of the people of Madagascar appear equal to their physical qualities, which are equal to those of other portions of the human race, yet they are generally characterized by apathy, want of decision, and excessive indolence. And these qualities, taken together with the oppression of the government, may be regarded as the fruitful source of much of the extreme poverty that prevails in the country, and of many of the seasons of famine from which they suffer so severely. The mass of the people seem alike destitute of forethought and en ...prise, and hence are unprepared for any failure of their crops, and unable to extricate themselves from any unforseen calamity. Nothing is a greater impediment to the advancement of civilization than indolence; and nothing shows this more distinctly than the state of starvation in which the people are sometimes found, while a small amount of labor on the rich soil of the country around them, would supply provisions in abundance for a greatly augmented population. They are also far from being cleanly in their persons, and bathe but seldom. They are not quick in avenging injuries, but cherish for a long time the desire of revenge for the most trifling insults, while they exult in the distress of others. The public executions exhibit more painfully, not only the absence of all the finer sensibilities of our nature, but the worse than brutalized state of the public mind. The unhappy victims of the treacherous ordeal of poisoned water which is used for detecting wickedness and witchcraft, are savagely dragged away, their bodies mutilat a most horrid manner, or they are hurled down a fearful precipice, in the presence of multitudes of spectators, who look on without the least emotion of pity; while the children who mingle with the crowd, amuse themselves by throwing stones at the lifeless bodies, which the dogs are rending to pieces. Yet this species of savagery would be likely to attend slave institutions, or a belief in witchcraft among any people.

They are exceedingly attached to their homes. The Hovas often, when setting out on a journey, take with them a small portion of their native earth, on which they often gaze when absent, and invoke their god that they may be permitted to return to restore it to the place from which it was taken. When returning from a foreign land to their native island, or from a distant province to their own, every countenance beams with gladness, they seem to be strangers to fatigue, and seek, by singing and dancing on their way, to give vent to the fullness of their joy.

It is curious to see how many traits in common these barbarous people have with those people of Christendom who boast of having the highest order of refinement and civilization. Duplicity is one of their most conspicuous traits of character. The natives will invent the most specious pretences, and assume the most plausible air, to impose on the credulity of others, and ingratiate themselves into favor, while their real designs are hid for weeks and months in their own bosoms. If they wish to make a request, they will preface it by so complimentary a speech, and so many thanks and blessings for a kindness yet to be done, and by such servile flattery for a virtue to be illustrated in the forth-coming gift, that one might imagine the whole nation a tribe of office seekers and politicians. It is often impossible to understand their object for an hour or more, as they will talk on the most apparently dissimilar subjects, but with a visible restlessness, until, after all the windings of plausability are traveled through, they hit, as if by accident, on the point designed from the beginning.

In bartering, every trader asks, at least, twice as much as he intends to take; and they never forget to boast of any instance of successful fraud. The best sign of genius in children is esteemed a quickness to deceive, over-reach, and cheat. The people delight in fabulous tales, but in none so much or universally as those that relate instances of successful deceit or fraud, though involving loss of life, as well a property, to the injured person.

2

Falsehood is a common vice among all. To lie, is esteemed clever and pleasant, and more likely to serve one's purpose of interest or pleasure than to tell the truth. Their constant aim in business is to swindle, in professed friendship to extort, and in mere conversation to exaggerate and fabricate. The laws regard the testimony of witnesses as mere circumstantial evidence. There seems to be no idea of vice unless it is defined by law. Their sensuality is universal and gross, though generally concealed; continence is not supposed to exist in either sex before marriage, consequently it is not expected, and its absence is not regarded as a vice.

Many of the Malagasy seem to think that expediency alone determines the character of actions, and act as if they had no conception of what is vicious. But while they regard theft and other acts of darker moral turpitude as almost harmless, innumerable, unmeaning ceremonies, such as abstaining from this or that habit, or from sitting in this or that particular posture, are enjoined as a duty and the neglect of them regarded as criminal. And in this respect the degeneracy of civilized man touches hands with the barbarian. Involved in the snaky folds of our own cunning, we forget the necessity of moral principle, and ascribe all our calamities to the departure from some mere expediency, and seek to attain to all good by external and demonstrational observances, which are often puerile and absurd, and worse than useless to those who perform them.

The Malagasy are also great talkers and speech-makers. Often even when about to cross a river they have to make a long oath, or enter into an engagement, to acknowledge the sovereignty of the crocodile in his own element, and make a speech to deprecate his ire. An instance is related of an old man, who, having spent nearly half an hour upon the banks of a river in pronouncing an oath, then addressed the crocodile in "a neat and appropriate speech," urging him to do him no injury, because he had never done him, the crocodile, any; assuring him that he had never engaged in war with any of his species; but on the contrary, that he had always entertained the highest veneration for him, and if he came to attack him, sooner or later vengeance would follow, for all his relatives and friends would declare war against him. After about a quarter of an hour of such speechifying as this, the old man then plunged into the stream, feeling as fully assured, probably, that he had averted an impending evil, as modern speech-makers often do when they descend from the stump.

CHAPTER III.

The manners and customs of the Malagasy are interesting as being chiefly of native growth, and as showing the strange developments of the human mind when not directed by those moral axioms whose exercise are absolutely essential to the higher order of civilization. Even before the birth of an infant there are ceremonies in anticipation of "the hour of nature's sorrow," which are as unmeaning as they are unnecessary. After the birth, the friends and relatives of the mother visit her, and offer their congratulations. The infant also receives salutations, in form resembling the following: "Saluted be the offspring given of God!—may the child live long!—may the child be favored so as to possess wealth!" Presents are made to the attendants in the household, and sometimes a bullock is killed and distributed among the members of the family. Presents of poultry, fuel, money, etc., are at times also sent by friends to the mother. A fire is kept in the room day and night, frequently for a week after the birth of a child. After this period the child is taken out of the house by some person whose parents are both living, and then taken back to the mother. In being carried out and in the child must be carefully lifted over the fire, which for this purpose is placed near the door. Should the infant be a boy, the ax, large knife, and spear, generally used in the family, must be taken out at the same time, with any implements of building that may be in the house. Silver chains, of native manufacture, are also given as presents, or used in these ceremonies, for which no particular reason is assigned.

One of the first steps of the father, or a near relative, is to report the birth of the child to the native divines or astrologers, who are required to work the *Sikidy* for the purpose of ascertaining and declaring its destiny. The Sikidy consists in mixing together a number of beans and small stones, and from the figures which they form, predicting either favorable or unfavorable results. If the destiny is declared to be favorable, the child is nurtured with that tenderness and affection which nature inspires, and the warmest congratulations are tendered by the friends of the parents.

At the expiration of the second or third month from the birth of the child a ceremony called "scrambling" takes place. A mixture of beef tallow, with rice, milk, honey, a sort of grass, and a lock of the infant's hair is cooked together in a rice pan, and when it is done, a general rush takes place upon the pan, and a scramble after its contents, especially by the women, as it is thought that those who are fortunate enough to get a portion may hope to become mothers.

With respect to names for children, these are bestowed without ceremony, and are generally descriptive, as they usually are among uncivilized tribes.

When the destiny of the child is pronounced unfavorable by the Sikidy, it is generally exposed to death, or else murdered outright, although an offering may sometimes avert the evil. The exposure is usually effected in this way: An infant—a new-born, perfectly helpless, unconscious infant—smiling perhaps in innocence, is laid on the ground in the narrow entrance to a village or cattle yard, through which there is but just room enough for cattle to pass; several cattle are then driven violently in, and are made to pass over the spot where the child is placed, while the parents stand by with agonizing feelings waiting the result.

If the oxen pass over without injuring the infant, the omen is propitious, the powerful and evil destiny is removed, the parents may without apprehension embrace their offspring and cherish it as one rescued from destruction. But should the child be crushed to death by the feet of the oxen, which is likely to be the case, the parents return to mourn their loss in the bitterness of grief, with no other consolation than that which the monstrous absurdities of their delusions supply—that, had their beloved infant survived, it would have been exposed to the influence of that destiny which now required its exposure to destruction.

In this sacrifice of infant life the radical idea would not seem to be greatly different from that which led to the worship of Moloch, in which human beings were offered to a god in the form of an ox, the ox being a principal source from which our physical life is derived and maintained. If we derive our life or sustenance from the ox, it seems fair to give to it of our human life in return. Such would seem to be the darkling mode of reasoning that leads barbarous nations to the practice of infanticide.

But there is a gloomier cast still to the divinations by the Sikidy, where the child is doomed to inevitable death, without the possibility of escape. When this inhuman decision of the astrologers has been announced, the death of the innocent victim is usually effected by suffocation, The infant's head is held with its face downwards in the rice pan filled with water, till life becomes extinct. Sometimes a piece of cloth is placed on the child's mouth, to render its suffocation more speedy. The remains of the infant thus murdered, are buried on the south side of the parents' house, that being superstitiously regarded as the part which is ill omened and fatal. The parents then rub a small quantity of red earth into their clothes, and afterwards shake them, as if to avert or shake off from themselves the evil supposed to be incurred by their slight and transient contact with that which had been doomed to destruction.

Another mode of perpetrating this unnatural deed is by taking the infant to a retired spot in the neighborhood of the village, digging a grave sufficiently large to receive it, pouring in a quantity of water slightly warmed, putting a piece of cloth on the infant's mouth, placing it in the grave, filling this up with earth, and leaving the helpless child thus buried alive, a memorial of their own affecting degradation, and the relentless barbarism of their gloomy superstition. Yet such seems to be one of the natural traits of man in his native condition, and wherein does it differ from the unconscious act of the crocodile in devouring its own young? Nature has thus constituted man; and it would seem as if besides the deadly fever, and frequent wars between hostile tribes, she had provided additional means to check the tendency to a superabundant overgrowth of population in one of her fertile tropical islands.

When the Malagasy child has escaped all the dangers to which its infant life is exposed, it is then beloved with additional tenderness by its parents. At a very early age, frequently before the sixth or seventh year is completed, girls and boys engage in the occupations of their parents respectively. The amusements of the children resemble on a smaller scale those of the adults. Bull-fighting is one of those held in the highest estimation among the latter; and children spend many hours in setting beetles to fight, and watching them while employed in destroying each other.

Children are betrothed at a very early age, and they marry at 12 and 14, becoming parents soon afterwards. There are certain degrees of relationship within which the laws prohibit marriage. The marriage ceremonies are very simple, and not very uniform. Great feasting takes place; the betrothed couple appear in their best dress, and their friends and relatives meet at the houses of the parents of the two parties. At the appointed hour, the relatives or friends of the bridegroom accompany him to the house of the bride. These either pay or receive the dowry agreed upon; he is welcomed by the bride as her future husband; they eat together, are recognized by the senior members of the family as husband and wife, a benediction is pronounced upon them, and a prayer offered to God that they may have a numerous offspring, abundance of cattle, many slaves, great wealth, and increase the honor of their respective families.

Polygamy is common among the Malagasy, the only restrictions upon it being that no man shall take twelve wives except the sovereign. There are many more ceremonies attending the taking of a second wife than the first, which it is needless to mention. The very name by which polygamy is designated—famporafesana, that is, "the means of causing enmity," implies the evils of which it is the fruitful source. It is the chief cause of nearly all the domestic disputes and jealousies existing among the Malagasy; wives become jealous of each other, and the husband suffers from the jealousy of all. In a word, polygamy is a curse to the land, and its final extinction is a consummation devoutly to be desired by all who prefer peace to wrath, affection to bitterness, domestic comfort to domestic strife, and Christian virtues to the jealousy, malice, and uncharitableness of the excited and turbulent passions of depraved human nature. It is a cause, among other evils, of numerous divorces. The divorced woman can marry again in twelve days, though it is possible for the husband to give a divorce of such a character that she can never marry again.

A widow forfeits all claim to respectability of character if she marry within twelve months of her husband's decease, and would, were she thus to act, be marked and shunned in society.

The ceremony of circumcision has been long practiced in the island, and as no one seems to know whence it came, it may possibly be regarded as indigenous. It dose not appear to have much religious significance, but would seem rather to be a mark of manhood, and to be more assimilated to the ceremony observed on assuming the *toga virilis* among the Romans, than to the institution of circumcision as practiced by the Semitic race. If the Malagasy are asked why they practice it, their answer is, because their ancestors did. And when asked why their ancestors did it, they reply, "Who can tell that?"

The time of performing this ceremony does not depend upon any particular age of the child, but upon the will of the sovereign, who, in consequence of an application from parents and friends of any number of children, appoints a time and orders the observance of the rite.

Great preparations are made for the occasion; the women plait their hair and ornament their persons, oxen are slayed for a feast, and chanting and singing and feasting are observed for a week preceding the ceremony. A calabash or gourd, for holding the holy water used on the occasion, is taken to the king or his representative for consecration, in which a large procession in the fullest ornament and dress is formed. In consecrating the gourd, the King, holding a shield in his left hand and a spear in his right, imitates the action of a warrior, and exhorts the fathers of those children who are about to undergo the rite, to enforce upon their attention the duty of loyalty and devotedness to their sovereign, that they may serve, honor, and do homage to him.

The vessel having been duly consecrated by the King's striking off with his spear the top of the gourd and binding it with plaits of a particular kind of grass and herbs, it is borne in procession, amidst dancing and shouting to the fields whence the water is to be taken. A stem of the banana-tree is planted there in the earth, and a tent is erected, wherein the party remain for the night. A fatted ram, purchased for the occasion, is killed and eaten with bananas, sugar-cane, etc., during the time the party is waiting for the sacred water.

While one party is procuring the holy water, another party is preparing the house in which the chief part of the rite is to be performed. All the furniture, the cooking utensils, and the mats, are removed, and the inside of the house hung with new mats to the very roof. A distribution of bullocks, sheep, poultry, rice, fruit, and vegetables is also made to the strangers who may be visiting at the time, and thus the day on which the party goes for the holy water ends.

As soon as the morning dawns, those lodging in the fields proceed to the pool whence the water is to be taken, and when they reach its margin, one of their number whose parents are both living descends into the water with the gourd in his hand and lowers himself in the water until the vessel is filled. Another standing opposite to him poising a spear, hurls it as if intending to kill him, but takes care merely to strike the earth near the place where he stands. This part of the ceremony may remind the reader of that passage in the Scripture where it is stated that God met Moses in the way and sought to kill him. When the calabash is filled with water, the bearer leaves the pool, and the procession moves towards the village, decorated with all the ornaments and finery which those who compose it have been able to procure. Stems of the banana-tree, ripe bananas, sugar-canes, bamboos, small canes, and silver chains, with various articles used during the ceremonies are also borne in the procession.

From day-light in the morning those in the village are all astire in preparing to go forth to meet the procession. Both sexes are ornamented with gold and silver chains, trinkets, silken robes, etc. Dollars, strung together by means of a strong line passed through holes near their edges, are worn like bands or fillets on the heads of the females, and over the shoulders of the men. This latter ornament is used as an indication of the wealth of the wearers or their families. In the procession, fathers take precedence, mothers follow, and friends and relatives bring up the rear. At about half a mile from the village they met those bringing the sacred water. The latter procession advances slowly, singing and dancing, and the leader, with his spear and shield, asks,—"What water is this?" The females then advance dancing, and sing—"Bless the water, the consecrated water that wearies."

On reaching the village, the whole procession moves three times round the house where the ceremony is to be performed, bearing the holy water and its accompaniments; after which they enter the house and wait till the amusements commence. They consist of bull-baiting, dancing, singing, beating drums, etc., and are kept up by alternate parties with considerable energy and hilarity until about sunset, when the people again enter the house. There, the females employ themselves in plaiting split rushes, for the purpose of forming small baskets. They sing and chant during the time they are thus employed; and the baskets, when finished, are suspended in a line extending northward, the basket intended for the eldest child being placed first.

While the females are employed making the baskets, the master of ceremonies kills a sheep in front of his house. This is called fahazza, "causing fruitfulness." After cutting off the head of the animal, the body is given to the multitude, who scramble for it, and in a few minutes tear the whole to pieces. The use of a knife or any sharp instrument is forbidden. Every female obtaining a portion is supposed to obtain fruitfulness with it. No sheep, however, possesses this potent efficacy, that is not of a certain kind and color, decided by the Sikidy.

The boys on whom the rite is to be performed are next led across the blood of the animal just killed, to which some idea of sacredness is attached. They are then placed on the west side of the house, and as they stand erect, a man, holding a light cane in his hand, measures the first child to the crown of the head, and at one stroke cuts off a piece of the cane measured to that height, having first dipped the knife in the blood of the slaughtered sheep. This knife is again dipped in the blood, and the child measured to the waist, when the cane is cut at that height. He is afterwards measured to the knee with similiar observances. The same ceremony is performed on all the children successively. The meaning of this, if indeed it has any meaning at all, seems to be the symbolical removal of all evils to which the child might be exposed—first, from the head to the waist, then from the waist to the knees, and finally from the knees to the sole of the foot.

A hole is now dug in the northeast corner of the house, in which a stem of the banana-tree is planted, and on it an earthen lamp is fixed to burn during the night. Great attention is paid to the fixing of the stem, that the height may be proper, and the lamp made fast. The stem of the banana is consecrated by water sweetened with honey, being poured into the hole and upon the stem. Large silver chains are placed in a rice-pan, and a portion of the sacred water and honey is poured upon them, by which they are supposed to be consecrated for the ceremony. Rice powder is also introduced. A small quantity of the honey and water is then given to each of the children, and the person presenting it pronounces benedictions on them, the silver chains in the meantime being rattled in the rice-pan. The benedictions are of this kind: "May the children prosper in the world!—may they have spacious houses well filled with silver and slaves!—may their cattle be too numerous for their folds, and may their property be great!—if stones are thrown at them may they not be hurt, and when stoning others may they hit!—if attempted to be seized, may they escape!—and if seizing others, may they catch!—if pursued by others may they not be caught, and if pursuing others may they overtake!—and may they be beloved by the King and people!"

These benedictions are repeated several times; and the people all the while repeat the national sound, " oo, oo, oo," in one continued note, as long as the breath can sustain it. This is a usual expression of pleasure, the significant sound of approbation, and conveys as much to the Malagasy as the heartiest thrice-repeated cheer does to the Englishman.

It is also repeatedly asked during this part of the ceremony —"Is it not well ? Is it not admirably well ? Is it not good ?" with many other equally important inquiries.

Having advanced thus far, some one, accustomed to speak in the public assemblies of the people, then addresses all who attend on the occasion, and charges them to behave with proper decorum during the proceedings, to avoid levity of conduct, and to enter the house with their heads uncovered, lest by any neglect or impropriety they should desecrate what is holy, and so render unavailing the ceremony. The lamp is then lighted, the drums beat, and dancing and singing commence, which are continued during the whole night.

The next morning the fathers of the children who are to be circumcised, fetch the baskets plaited on the preceding day, and in which bananas are placed as offerings to avert future evils. These offerings (called Faditra) are placed first on the children, and are then carried away by the fathers, who prostrate themselves, as they leave the house, at a spot a short distance from the village, where they are cast away. No one dares to touch these bananas; they are deemed accursed, and are devoted to bearing away evil.

The ceremony of fetching the Ranomahery "strong water" now takes place. Early in the morning the double calabash is brought out of the house, a hole is struck through the center, and silver chains are put in. It is then carried to a running stream, and carefully filled by passing the vessel up the stream in a sloping direction, that the water may flow into it. In fetching it, the bearers must run with the utmost rapidity, having first girded up their loins. The leader of this party also carries a spear and a shield. The people collect at the entrance of the village, and await the return of the water-bearers, each one holding reeds and stones in his hands, with which, in a playful manner, they pretend to assault the water bearers on their return. A song is repeated on this occasion, consisting of these few simple expressions—Zana boro mahary Manatody ambato—"the young eagle lays her eggs on the rock;" implying, that in like manner the children will attain places now deemed inaccessible, and deposit their property beyond the reach of danger and spoliation. After walking round the house three times as before, the party enters, bending forward as they approach the door.

A young bullock of red color, selected for the occasion, being now brought into the court-yard of the house, the person who is to perform the rite advances, cuts a slit in the animal's ear, and dips his knife in the blood which flows therefrom. At the dropping of the blood from the ear of the animal, the children are supposed to be placed under a guarantee from future harm. A small drum is then placed near the threshold of the door, and the boy on whom the ceremony is now to be performed, being seated upon it, is firmly held by several men, and his ears stopped by those around him. The father stands close to the door outside, with his spear in his right hand and his shield in the left, performing with them the actions of a warrior; and while at this moment the act is performed, the father exclaims: ''Thou art become a man, mayst thou be loved—loved by the sovereign and by the people!—may the sovereign continue to reign long!—may there be mutual confidence between thee and the people!—be of good report among the people!—be facile of instruction, and of a docile disposition!'' The father exhorts the child to take courage, declaiming, that now he has become a man, he should have a gun, a spear, and a shield, and should follow the King; that now he belonged to the King, he should henceforth serve him, and do homage to him, but that if he cried, he should not be the child of the King, but would be stigmatized as effeminate, and respected by no one.

The rano mahery, "strong water," is immediately employed in washing the children. While the rite is performing, the mothers are crawling about on the floor, touching the earth with their hands, and throwing dust and ashes on their hair, as tokens of humiliation on account of their children. Each mother rises from the ground at the moment her child has received the rite, and endeavors to assuage its grief, nursing it beside the fire.

The rite being thus performed, there is usually a distribution made by the chiefs of the district, and by the heads of families, of a number of oxen, to be killed and divided among the strangers and visitors. The parties then return to their several homes, when a fowl is killed, and some bananas are given to the children. In the course of two or three weeks the whole ceremony terminates by feasting, and rude signs of rejoicing, accompanied with dancing and singing.

Another popular institution of the Malagasy is that of forming *Brotherhoods*, which is a species of masonry, though it does not appear to be based upon secrecy. Its object is to form a strict bond of friendship between two or more individuals, and is called fatidra, *i.e.*, "dead blood," either because the binding oath is taken over the blood of a fowl killed on the occasion, or because a small portion of blood is drawn from each individual when thus pledging friendship, and drunk by those to whom friendship is pledged, with execrations of vengeance on each other, in case of violating the sacred oath.   To obtain this blood, a slight incision is made in the skin covering the center of the bosom, significantly called ambarafo, "the mouth of the heart."

There are many ceremonies connected with the formation of this bond of brotherhood, all of which are designed to impress upon the minds of those entering upon it the sanctions of the oaths which are taken.   These brotherhoods are not sufficiently numerous in their membership to prove dangerous to society or to the government, and are beneficial to the individuals who belong to them.   They are specially beneficial to the slaves, between whom the obligations can be formed as well as between their masters.

This engagement of brotherhood, accompanied with solemn oaths and the drinking of each other's blood, has also been observed to prevail in the Island of Borneo; and this fact furnishes another evidence besides a common language, that the people of Madagascar have some affinity, not understood, with those who inhabit the wide-spread islands of Polynesia.

It is needless to enter into details with respect to the character of slavery in Madagascar, since it resembles in so many particulars the institution as recently witnessed among ourselves. Its mingled guilt, degradation and misery are the same there as they have been among us, and from which, long years, and perhaps still farther suffering and bloodshed, will be necessary to enable us to recover, and to place ourselves once more upon that elevated and Christian ground upon which we began our national career.

Some of the nobles possess several hundred slaves each, and these are employed in all the varied ways, and under similar conditions that they were formerly in the United States.

Like all other barbarous people, the Malagasy are generous

and hospitable, their own modes of living being so miserable that they are very willing to share freely with others. Where people rely upon the spontaniety of nature, or upon the labor of slaves for their food and shelter, it becomes an easy matter to manifest the ruder semblances of hospitality; but as for imparting Christian solace and comfort they know nothing. These they rather persecute and expel.

Should one be content to dine on locusts and silk worms, he could be highly entertained. Large swarms of locusts are often seen in Madagascar in the spring and summer. They generally approach from the southwestern quarter of the island, and pass like a desolating scourge over the face of the country, leaving trees and shrubs entirely leafless, and destroying the plantations of rice and manioc, and whatever the gardens contain. Their appearance on approaching is like a dense cloud of considerable extent, the lowest part of which is about two feet above the ground, while the upper part rises to a great elevation. The natives, on the approach of the locusts, fly to their gardens, and, by noises and shouts of the most tumultuous kind, endeavor to prevent their alighting. In the uncultivated parts of the country they often dig holes, of large dimensions, and nearly a foot deep, in which great quantities are collected and taken; or they arrest them in their flight by wide shallow baskets, or by striking them down with their lambas, after which they are gathered up in baskets by women and children. The locusts form at times an important element of food; for this purpose they are caught as above described, slightly cooked, and eaten, after the legs and wings have been picked off; or they are partially boiled in large earthen or iron vessels, dried in the sun, and repeatedly winnowed, in order to clear the bodies from the legs and wings; they are afterwards packed up in baskets, and carried to the market for sale, or kept in large sacks or baskets in the house for domestic use, similarly to the manner practiced by the Indians who inhabit the deserts of Utah.

Locusts are usually cooked by frying them in an iron or earthen vessel; and the natives say that they resemble shrimps.

Silk worms, in the chrysalis state, are also cooked and eaten. Considerable quantities of them are gathered in several provinces of the island, where the *tapia edulis* grows, the plant on which the silk worms feed, and are exposed for sale in the markets.

How long the art of distillation has been known in the island, cannot be ascertained; but spirituous liquors are made from sugar-cane, honey, berries, and other native productions. French wines are also known; and as a caution to etymologists it may be-stated that the native word for wine is "divray," which one might be slow to expect to come from the French *du vin*. This native word hardly resembles its original so nearly as Vazimba would the word Mitzraim, the name for the ancient Egyptians, between which, however, there may be no connection.

The greatest scourges that afflict the island in the form of disease are fever and the small-pox. This latter disease is so much dreaded by the natives that they have been known to drive away and kill with stones one who may first become attacked by it. Thousands have been swept off by it at a time. With respect to the fever, which seldom prevails in the highlands, the best time for Europeans to land upon the island is in the months of July, August and September.

The ceremónials attending the burial of the dead are numerous and interesting; but we confine ourselves to a passing notice. The Malagasy, like the Jews and some other nations, attach ideas of uncleanness or pollution to touching a corpse. No corpse is permitted to be carried to the grave along the principal thoroughfare of the capital, which is thought to be in some measure sacred. Nevertheless the same street is sometimes stained with the blood of human victims destroyed in obedience to false and cruel divinations. No one who has attended a funeral is permitted to enter into the court-yard of the palace till eight days have elapsed, and then he must bathe before he can be admitted. In all cases, a total or partial ablution of the garments of the mourners must take place on return from the grave.

The tombs of the Malagasy are placed sometimes in front of their houses, or occupy a place by the road-side. At others, they are built in the midst of a village, or where two roads meet. Often a person begins to erect his tomb in early life, and makes its completion through a series of years one of the most important objects of his existence, deeming a costly repository for his mouldering remains the most effectual remedy of being held in honorable remembrance by posterity. In constructing a tomb, a large excavation is made in the earth, and the roofs and sides of the vault are made of immense slabs of stone. Incredible labor is often employed in bringing these slabs from a distance to the spot where the tomb is to be constructed. The sides of a vault six or seven feet high, and ten or twelve feet square, are often formed of single stones of these dimensions. A sort of subterraneous room is thus built; which, in some parts of the country, is lined with rough pieces of timber. The stones are covered with earth, to the depth of from fifteen to eighteen inches. This mass of earth is faced with a curb of stone, and upon this a second and third mound or mass of earth is formed, each of smaller dimensions than the lowest one, but faced with stone in the same way, and being from twelve to eighteen inches in height, thus forming altogether a flat pyramidal mass, composed of successive terraces, and resembling in appearance the pyramidal structures of the aborigines of South America. They are, indeed, like the rough state of the Egyptian pyramids as they are supposed to have been before the last exterior coating of stone was added in order to render the pyramidal slant unbroken and complete. The summit of the grave is ornamented with large pieces of rose or white quartz. The stone-work exhibits, in many instances, very good workmanship, and reflects great credit on the skill of the native masons. Some of these rude structures are stated to be twenty feet in width, and fifty feet long.

The large slabs used in forming the tombs, as described, are usually of granite or sienite. The natives have long known how to detach blocks of stone from the mountain mass by means of burning cow-dung on the part they wish to remove, and dashing cold water along the line on the stone they have heated. Having been thus treated, the stone easily separates in thick layers, and is forced up by means of levers. Mysterious "odies," or charms, are employed in marking out the desired dimensions of the slab, and to their virtue is foolishly attributed the splitting of the stone, though they well know that all the "odies" in the island could not split a stone unless heat were applied. Yet this is a species of *speculative* masonry which appears to belong to the recondite art of stone-work. When the slab is detached, bands of straw are fastened round it, to prevent breakage in the removal. Strong ropes are attached to the slab, and, amidst the boisterous vociferations of the workmen, it is dragged away from the quarry. In ascending a hill, wooden rollers are placed under the stone, and moved forward as it advances.

Sometimes five or six hundred men are employed in dragging a single stone. A man usually stands on the stone, acting as director. He holds a cloth in his hand, and waves it with loud and incessant shouts, to animate those who are dragging the ponderous block. At his shouting they pull in concert, and so far his shouting is of real service. Holy water is also sprinkled on the stone as a means of facilitating its progress, till at length, after immense shouting, sprinkling, and pulling, it reaches its destination.

When the tomb is erected for a person deceased, but not yet buried, no noise is made in dragging the stones for its construction. Profound silence is regarded as indicating the respect of the parties employed. The tombs are occasionally washed with a mixture of lime, or white clay, and thus furnish to the eye of the traveler a pleasing variety in the objects around him. The entrance to the vault is covered by a large upright block of stone, which is removed when a corpse is taken in, and fixed in its former position at the termination of the ceremony. Small native fans are used in driving insects from the corpse, while it remains in the house, and on the road to the grave; these are left stuck in the earth over the grave. High poles are often planted around the tomb, upon which the skulls and horns of the bullocks slaughtered at the interment are stuck, the number of these showing the wealth of the family, or the value of the tribute thus rendered by survivors to the memory of the departed. Sometimes the horns are stuck in the earth at the corners of the tomb, or fixed in the form of a fence around it. This is considered highly ornamental.

Those who are desirous of paying great respect to their deceased relatives, and of preserving their tombs in good repair, keep the ground immediately around the graves in neat and excellent order, preserving it perfectly smooth and level, and free from weeds. In the tombs of the wealthy much treasure is often buried.

Though the Malagasy are exceedingly kind and attentive to their sick, and exhibit the most grand and solemn manifestations of respect on the death of noted persons among them, yet they leave the bodies of criminals at the foot of the precipice from which they have been thrown, to be torn to pieces by the dogs, and to litter the earth with their bones.

Some of the amusements of the Malagasy are quite curious. The wife in saluting her husband, or the slave his master, on his return from war or from a journey, crawls on the ground and licks his feet.

One of their common amusements is to form themselves into two parties in order to abuse each other in the most violent language that their imaginations can invent; and those who excel in the most abusive vituperation, obtain the plaudits of the spectators.

Another game is called Mamely dia manga, "kicking backwards," or, what may be literally translated, "striking blue with the sole of the foot." The game consists in two parties kicking each other in the same manner as horses, asses, or other animals. This accomplishment is sedulously cultivated, from youth to manhood, and many become desperately expert at it, broken ankles and legs often being the consequences. Hundreds at a time occasionally join in this rude sport, forming themselves into parties on opposite sides and driving at each other with amazing force, each seeking to maintain its advanced position and repel its antagonist by kicking backwards.

One of the most abhorrent customs of the Malagasy is the administration of a poison called the *tangena*, for the purpose of expelling wickedness and witchcraft. The tangena is an exceedingly poisonous nut of the *Tanghinia Veneniflua* which grows in the island. In order to ascertain whether any one is overwicked, or practices witchcraft, three pieces of skin from a fowl's back are taken, and the nut scraped into them in a fine powder; they are then rolled up, and the suspected person is made to swallow them. The poison acts as a powerful emetic; and if all the pieces of skin are thrown up the accused is acquitted; but otherwise he is condemned and executed. Sometimes permission is granted by the sovereign to administer it to the persons of a whole district at a time, and it is performed with a degree of barbarous and absurd ceremony, with an air of mysterious solemnity, and at the same time with such a horrid destruction of human life, as to cause one to contemplate it with a shudder of the deepest disgust. So savage do the people become under the influence of this abominable ceremony, that they shun their own relations who become accused, and not unfrequently the unfortunate victim who fails to vomit up the three pieces of skin, is hurried while yet alive, to his grave, and is thrown in and there crushed by the stones that are piled upon him. Nothing could compare with the monstrous deformity of this custom, in civilized countries, unless it was the ante de fe of Spain, or the incidental burning of slaves in the United States; and one looks on in wonder at the darkling operations of the human mind when not aided by power from an outer source beyond itself.

The Sikidy, or process of divination, we have already mentioned. It is regarded with the greatest popular favor, and is used on all occasions. It shows how prone the Malagasy mind is to rely upon some power beyond its own reason, and is an indication of the great facility with which they meght be led, if properly managed, to accept the tenets of the Christian religion. Such rank superstition may be regarded as a rich, tropical soil, in which an enlightened faith might be trained to grow in the greatest perfection.

The directions of the oracle called the Sikidy respect two different kinds of offerings; the *sorona* being intended to obtain favors, and the *faditra* to avert evils. Both, perhaps, partake more of the nature of charms than strictly of sacrifices, and the *sorona* especially. The *faditra* is a thing rejected; and in throwing it away, the offerer believes he averts some dreaded evil. There is, in this ceremony, something analagous to the institution among the ancient Jews, of sending away into the wilderness the scape-goat, bearing on its head the weight and curse of the confessed iniquities of the congregation of Israel. The material of the ceremony differs, and so does the mode, but the spirit and design have a resemblance; and hence the idea which first occurs to a Malagasy, in connection with such texts of Scripture as represent Christ bearing the sins of the world, is that of a powerful *faditra*—the taking away of evil—the averting of suffering or death.

CHAPTER IV.

We have thus given but an imperfect outline of the character of the population of the island as exhibited in their pagan condition. Numerous illustrations of their condition and modes of life, of a highly entertaining nature, might de added, but we have presented enough to enable the reader to form some idea of the state of the island at the time when, at the close of the French revolution, the English authorities at the Mauritius began a systematic course of action to introduce the benefits of Christian civilization, To this end, the Governor of Mauritius and its dependencies, Sir Robert Farquhar, directed his first efforts towards the suppression of the foreign slave-trade of Madagascar. The particular juncture of affairs in the island was propitious. The king of the Hovas, Radama, had succeeded to his father, whose intentions had been to bring all the tribes of the island under his own sway, and thus to establish but one government for the whole country. The son, Radama, proved to be a worthy successor of such a sire. He was warlike, enterprising, intelligent, eager for instruction, and was taking lessons in French, having already learned to write his own language in the Arabic character. But the objects of the English governor are so lucidly explained in his own words, that we can do no better than to give these words themselves. In a letter from the Mauritius dated September 12th, 1816 to Earl Bathurst, Governor Farquhar says:—

" I beg leave to state to your lordship the arrival, in this island, of two young brothers of Radama, King of the Orahs, the most powerful of the princes of Madagascar; an event which may be of considerable importance to the inhabitants of these colonies, and which may be followed by advantageous results for the ultimate civilization of Madagascar.

" The different chiefs and sovereigns of the island had been inspired with much jealousy and distrust of the British government, by the artifices of such of the French traders as had been interested in the slave-trade, and whose traffic was suppressed by the establishment of the British government in these islands.

" I therefore thought it indispensably necessary for preserving the harmony which should subsist between the British merchants and other subjects settled at Madagascar, and the native princes, to send a person properly qualified to the latter, in the hopes of forming a lasting peace, and procuring protection to his Majesty's subjects in that island.

" One of his Majesty's subjects, a Frenchman, of the name of Chardeneaux, was indicated to me as peculiarly adapted for the accomplishment of this service, from his long and intimate acquaintance with the different native chiefs, and particularly from the friendship which had subsisted between him and Radama, King of the Orahs, for many years.

" As my desire was, at the same time, to endeavor, by every amicable means, to cut off one great source of supply for the slave-traffic, and as such a mission would at first appear as eminently embracing the interests of the native princes, I was the more disposed to accept the services of M. Chardeneaux on this occasion.

"Subjoined is the copy of a private instruction on this head, which I furnished to M. Chardeneaux, and his answer.

"Of the brothers of Radama, now arrived here, one is the presumptive heir of his authority; they are accompanied by two of the chief ministers of their prince, by a son of one of the nobles of the nation of Betanininies, three ministers of the King of Tamatavé, two chieftains of the South, and a numerous suite.

"We have reason to look on the persons now here, on the part of their respective sovereigns of Madagascar, as representing all that is powerful in the center and on the coasts of that vast island.

"Of these sovereigns, the most warlike, most intelligent, and possessing the greatest means, is Radama. His people are the most industrious, and further advanced in the arts of life than any other nation of Madagascar; and he has incorporated into the mass of his subjects, and reduced to his authority, all the surrounding petty States; his army consists of 40,000 men, armed with fire-arms.

"It therefore appears that the friendship of so powerful a chieftain cannot fail in being eminently useful in assuring the safety, and facilitating the commerce which may be undertaken with a view of replacing that traffic in slaves abolished by the legislature.

"These friendly bonds will, no doubt, be strengthened, and the prospect of growing civilization opened, by the opportunity now given to the young princes to learn the arts and customs of European life, and the principles of our religion.

"The king Radama is himself eager for instruction; writes his language in Arabic character, and is learning to write French in Roman letters. His brothers, who are arrived here, appear very intelligent for their age, which is about nine or ten years, and capable of acquiring every requsite principle of morals and religion.

"There is a British missionary here, of the name of Le Brun, who has been remarkably successful in the education of the numerous class of free colored people with which this island abounds; and he has conducted himself with so much discretion, as not to have given the smallest offence to any of the inhabitants, although his employment is of that nature to be viewed with jealousy by colonists in general. It is my intention to propose to this man to proceed to the court of Radama, and reside there; by which means I shall have constant communication with the interior of Madagascar, and be able to make the best use of the friendship of that prince, for the mutual interests of our respective countries.

"I trust your lordship will not disapprove of those peaceful and inexpensive overtures to a more constant and safer intercourse with the island of Madagascar; means of this nature will enable us to push our commerce further than the forts and garrisons which have hitherto afforded protection to the merchants who traded thither. The former governors of these islands have, in every period of their history, in vain endeavored to obtain that friendly footing which is now sought and offered to us by the native princes.

"I shall not intrude longer upon your lordship's time, by any exposition of the political value of Madagascar, as forming an appendage to the British sovereignty in these seas, as my former letters have been sufficiently explicit on that head; but I may be allowed to observe, that it appears to me, that the means are at present in our hands of cutting off, in a great measure, at its source, the slave-trade in these seas, and that I shall not neglect so favorable an opportunity of availing myself of them to the fullest extent."

Such were the means adopted to induce Radama to send over to Mauritius two of his younger brothers, Ratifikia and Rahovy, for the purpose of receiving an European education. At the close of the same year a mission was sent by Governor Farquhar, with the intention of forming a treaty of friendship and peace with Radama. The party sent for this purpose consisted of Captain Le Sage, as agent, a medical gentleman, about thirty soldiers, a Monsieur Jolicoeur as interpreter, several artificers who had been sent to Mauritius as convicts from India, Verkey, who was at that time in the employment of the traders, but afterwards sent to England, and some others. The soldiers were sent with a view of exhibiting to Radama the military manœuvres of disciplined European troops. A considerable number of this party unhappily fell victims to the Malagasy fever, in consequence of having traveled through the country during the rainy season, which has been found by experience to prove fatal. Yet notwithstanding a severe attack of this fever, Le Sage reached the capital, gave the presents with which he was charged to the King, Radama, and on the 14th of January, 1817, performed the ceremony of taking the oath of blood with that monarch. On the 4th of February following a treaty was concluded with which Le

Sage and his party set out on their return to Tamatavé, whence they set sail for Mauritius.

Mr. Brady and another soldier were left behind at the capital, by Radama's particular request, for the purpose of instructing his people in European tactics. The latter of the two soldiers rendered himself odious by his severity, not an uncommon fault from the Saxon race towards other races which they despise, unless controlled by a higher order of Christian sentiment than usually prevails among soldiers; but Mr. Brady secured the good-will of the natives, and continued long to enjoy the esteem both of the people and of their sovereign.

Although no plan for the abolition of the slave-traffic had yet been matured, yet care had been taken, by the proper arguments, to dispose the King's intelligent mind in its favor. The two youths, younger brothers of Radama, sent for education to Mauritius, were placed under the immediate superintendence of Mr. Hastie, with detailed instructions on the most enlightened principles, carefully drawn up by his Excellency the Governor of Mauritius. In the month of July, 1817, they returned to Tamatavé, accompanied by Mr. Hastie, and were received there by Radama himself, who had gone down to the coast at that period with about 30,000 of his people, partly for the purpose of receiving his brothers, and partly to suppress some provincial disturbances, as well as to form some political arrangements on the coast, and to prove that he was not "a beardless boy," as some of the chiefs of the island had called him.

Mr. Hastie took with him on this occasion some horses as a present to the King. He arrived in the capital on the 6th of August, 1817, and was received at Court as assistant agent with great demonstrations of favor, where the King appeared in a scarlet coat and military hat which had been sent to him from Mauritius, and in blue pantaloons and green boots. The King introduced to him Mr. Brady as his captain, and no longer a private soldier.

At length, on the 23rd of October, 1817, and after many difficulties had been overcome, a treaty was agreed upon between Governor Farquhar and King Radama, from which the following extracts are given in order to show its character:

"Article 2nd.—It is agreed, and the two contracting parties hereby covenant and agree, that, from the date of this treaty, there shall be an entire cessation and extinction, through all the dominions of King Radama, and wherever his influence can extend, of the sale or transfer of slaves, or other persons whatever, to be removed from off the soil of Madagascar, into any country, island, or dominion of any other prince, potentate, or power, whatever; and that Radama, King of Madagascar, will make a proclamation and a law, prohibiting all his subjects, or persons depending upon him, in his dominions, to sell any slave to be transported from Madagascar, or to aid, or abet, or assist in any such sale, under penalty that any person so offending shall be reduced to slavery himself.

" Article 3d.—And in consideration of this concession on the part of Radama, the king of Madagascar, and his nation, and in full satisfaction of the same, and for the loss of revenue thereby incurred by Radama, King of Madagascar, the commissioners, on the part of his Excellency the Governor of Mauritius, do engage to pay Radama, yearly, the following articles:

" One thousand dollars in gold; one thousand dollars in silver; one hundred barrels of powder, of 100 lbs. each; one hundred English muskets, complete, with accoutrements; ten thousand flints; four hundred red jackets; four hundred shirts; four hundred pairs of trowsers; four hundred pairs of shoes; four hundred soldiers' caps; four hundred stocks; twelve sergeants' swords (regulation) with belts; four hundred pieces of white cloth, two hundred pieces of blue cloth,—India; a full-dress coat, hat, and boots, all complete, for King Radama; two horses—upon a certificate being received, that the said laws and regulations, and proclamations, have been enforced the preceding quarter; which certificate shall be signed by King Radama, and countersigned by the agent of his Excellency, Governor Farquhar, resident at the Court of Radama."

Mr. Hastie hastened to Mauritius with this treaty, and arrived there on the 9th of November, just at the moment when his Excellency, the Governor, was embarking for England on a leave of absence. Mr. Hastie was appointed to see that the conditions of the treaty were duly observed by Radama, re-embarked the same day and returned to Tamatavé, where he found the slave-dealers already selling off their possessions, and preparing to leave Madagascar. The King issued a proclamation, preventing his people from being carried off the island into slavery, and prohibiting attacks being made upon the Sultan of Johanna and the Comoro Islands, for the purpose of getting slaves, under the penalties of piracy.

Thus far things had gone on well, under the direction of an

enlightened, philanthropic governor; but unhappily, the slave-
trade of Madagascar was not to die without a struggle, and as
is not unfrequently the case, its adherents found a powerful
ally in one whose duty it was to suppress it, and who occupied a position powerful for good or evil. That we may
give a clearer idea of how this event happened, we must make
a somewhat detailed statement.

As the first payment of the articles agreed upon in the
treaty was to become due in May, 1818, Mr. Hastie repaired to
Tamatavé, on his way to Mauritius, to get them. But what was
his disappointment to learn, by a vessel which arrived with
several slave-dealers on board, that the acting Governor of
Mauritius, Governor Hall, had relinquished farther intercourse with the chieftains of Madagascar, *that he refused to
pay the equivalent stipulated by Governor Farquhar*, and intended to recall the agent stationed at the capital. A letter
from the Governor at Mauritius was at the same time presented,
with much formality, to Mr. Hastie, by a *deputation of the
slave-dealers*, recalling him from Madagascar. The deputation,
having delivered the letter, put the taunting question—
"Who, did Mr. Hastie think, possessed the purer sense of
honor—*the enlightened English, or the savage Radama?*"

Governor Hall seems to have done his work radically. He
prohibited Missionaries, who had been sent out by the London
Missionary Society at the request of Governor Farquhar, from
proceeding to Madagascar, and he sent back to the island six
youths who had been under instruction in the Mauritius since
1817. At a later period, when efforts were resumed to mend
the serious mischief which Governor Hall had done, Radama
asked, "Why would not your government at Mauritius permit
these boys to be instructed, whom I had sent for that purpose? Although your government violated the treaty, and
discontinued intercourse with me, I would gladly have paid
for the education of the boys!"

Under the auspices of Governor Hall, Radama permitted
the slave-trade to recommence; and that it was again carried
on extensively, is obvious from General Hall's letter to the
Right Honorable Lord Bathurst, in 1818, wherein he states that,
"three cargoes had been imported during the preceding fort-
night, notwithstanding all his efforts to forbid such illegal
importation of slaves into the colony." The conduct of
Governor Hall brought lasting disgrace on the British name,
and added another to the melancholy catalogue of events

illustrative of the calamitous results of even temporary power in the hands of weak or wicked men. It is but due to the British government to state, that the conduct of the acting governor was severely condemned.

Governor Farquhar returned to the Mauritius in July, 1820, and soon took measures to repair the great injury done to the public service by Governor Hall; but it required much labor and pains to again restore Radama to his former confidence. " I am not independent," said he to Mr. Hastie. "The support of a King, is his subjects; and you have told me that unlimited power over them is not invested even in your civilized King, whose representative has occasioned me to risk my ascendency in Ankova. What am I to say to my subjects? They obtain everything they want by the sale of slaves; and how can I ask them to renew a treaty with a nation that has deceived them? They will naturally say, that I, individually, am to reap the benefit of it; and that stopping the trade will cause them, in a short time, to lose all the advantages they now derive from it."

However, the treaty was at length publicly renewed, and its execution this time was pursued with vigor and earnestness by both parties. This event took place on the 11th of Oct., 1820, and in describing it Mr. Hastie says—"The moment arrived when the welfare of millions was to be decided: I agreed! —and I trust that Divine Power which guides all hearts, will induce the government to sanction the act. The Kabary (council) was convened, the proclamation published, and received with transports by thousands. The British flag was unfurled; and freedom,—freedom from the bloody stain of slave dealing— hailed as the gift of the British nation. I declare," adds this generous-hearted man, "the first peal of Radama's cannon, announcing the amity sealed, rejoiced my heart more than the gift of thousands would have done."

The King forwarded orders for the immediate return of all slaves sent down to the coast and not then sold. He published an edict, that if any of his subjects were indebted to the slave-traders, they must without delay pay them in *money*, as on no pretext whatever could a deviation from his orders for the entire suppression of the slave-traffic meet a milder punishment than death. He at the same time sent off orders to Mazanga on the western coast, forbiding both the Arabs and natives there from carrying on the trade, although that part of the island had not yet acknowledged his sovereignty.

In the meantime the missionaries and soldiers were actively

engaged in performing their part of the work of civilization. The former had established schools which were largely attended, and on the part of the military an entire regiment had been modled and disciplined on the European system, by means of which the King was fast subduing the entire island to his single control. The Sakalavas, a powerful tribe of blacks, had formerly been the leading tribe of the island, but by means of the European system of tactics now used in the army of Radama, they were forced to succumb to his power.

A number of Malagasy youths were sent to England to be educated, two of whom were put into a government establishment to learn the art of making powder, while the others were confided to the care of the directors of the London Missionary Society, by whom they were placed under kind and attentive instructors. The King established a large school in the court-yard of his palace, consisting of officers of the army and their wives, who were instructed by his own secretary. The orthography of the language of the country was established, and by the authority of the King the English consonants and the French vowels were adopted. Mr. Hastie brought from Mauritius a band of music which had been instructed there. A printing press was finally introduced into the island, and in course of time large editions of spelling and other elementary books were printed, amounting to five thousand copies each, but yet not enough were supplied to meet the growing demand. The printing and book-binding of the mission was performed to a considerable extent by the natives, and no fewer than 15,000 copies, and portions of the Scriptures, and other books, were furnished, and upwards of six thousand of them put in circulation.

Among the useful arts and other elements of civilization introduced by the missionaries, not the least admirable one to the Malagasy was the horse. In consequence of the great care and kindness which the people bestowed upon the two horses that had been presented to the King, the animals began to suffer from being overfed on rice. It required all Mr. Hastie's skill to restore them to health; and when they were again in a condition to be used, the King asked to mount one of them. As soon as he was in the saddle he put a charm in his mouth in order to protect him against the dangers of his novel situation. This fear, however, soon abated, and nothing could exceed the joy and satisfaction that he evinced at having accomplished the feat of riding around the court-yard. He laughed loudly, screamed and danced, declaring that he had never received so much pleasure before. As he grew more accustomed to the exercise, his enjoyment of it every time increased; and like most learners who have attained a slight degree of proficiency, he evinced a consciousness of his own superiority, by wishing to see others placed in the situation which had lately appeared so perilous to him. Several of his officers were accordingly ordered to make the experiment, while he laughed heartily at their awkwardness.

But one day Radama fell from his horse, and, though not seriously injured, great confusion prevailed among the attendants on the King's person and the inmates of the palace. The domestics ran for the missionary, but were all too much alarmed to state what they wanted, or do more than inform him that the King was injured, and perhaps dying. Mr. Jones, the missionary, followed them and entered the palace, where the King was lying on the floor, his face and neck being covered with blood. Fearing the worst consequences from the loss of royal blood, especially if the supply was not kept up, a number of live fowls were brought, and some of the attendants were busily employed in cutting off the heads of the fowls, and and pouring the blood from their decapitated trunks into the King's mouth; others were making loud lamentations, embracing and kissing his feet; and others were fanning him, and wailing over him as already dead. Mr. Jones recommended their not adding any more blood from the fowls, and proposed instead to take some from the King. Violently opposing this, the attendants exclaimed,—"What! take away more blood, when the King has lost so much already! No,— let the *Sikidy* be consulted!" The King, though feeble, heard what was going on; and such was his confidence in the missionary, that he said, in a low tone, "Bleed me; let the Sikidy not be consulted: bleed me immediately." This the attendants refused to allow, and still continued cutting off the heads of the fowls, and pouring their blood into the King's mouth. Aided by Messrs. Robin and Brady, the King was placed in a chair facing the door, and Mr. Jones prepared to bleed him; but when about to open the vein, a principal officer standing by, seized his arm, and prevented it. Mr. Jones, however, kept his hand so firmly fixed, that the moment his right arm was released, he accomplished his purpose. When the blood appeared, a cry was raised to stop it. This was refused. The King fainted, and the cry was repeated with frantic distraction. Radama, however, soon revived, appeared better, and was put to rest. The *Sikidy* was then consulted, to ascertain who might enter the house, and approach his Majesty. The deviners declared that the Sikidy directed that none should enter but Mr. Jones, two other foreigners, and about twelve attendants, including the King's mother and three of his wives —the Sikidy evidently being shaped by the success already attained. The King continued to improve; and when the benefits resulting from bleeding were thus apparent, the people poured their benedictions on the missionary as heartily as they had before opposed him; and in order that the advantage might accrue to themselves also, they strongly solicited Mr. Jones to bleed them too, in anticipation of a fall, or other accident, which might render it necessary!

But at length, some years after this event, while the missionaries, aided by this strong-minded man, were in the full tide of successful effort, the King took sick and died. This melancholy event occurred on the 1st of August, 1828; and on the 3d of that month the official proclamation was made that the King " *had gone to his fathers.* "

He was succeeded in the kingdom by Ranavalona, his senior wife, and an enemy to the missionaries and Christianity.

The reign of Radama constitutes an epoch in the history of Madagascar, too important ever to be lost sight of. Important as regards its alliance with Great Britain, the suppression of the slave-trade, the adoption of a general system of education, and the introduction of Christianity into the very heart of the country ; while the subjugation of nearly the whole island, the formation of a large native army on the European model, the reduction of the language to considerable form and order, the establishment of a printing press at the capital, and the diffusion of numerous branches of art and science from enlightened countries, are events which give a marked character to that period, and to the history of the country, and of the sovereign under whose auspices they occurred.

In 1823 the King had visited Tamatavé with the expectation of meeting Sir Robert Farquhar there, but the Governor had already left on his way to England before the King's arrival. Proceeding to Foule Point he there had an interview with Captain Moorsom, of the British Man-of-War, Ariadne ; who, in return, invited him on board his vessel. English officers were left on shore as hostages, for he had some trouble to satisfy his people about his safety, the French having spread the report that the English were in the habit of entraping chiefs on board their ships and carrying them off.

"Radama," says Captain Moorsom, "is an extraordinary man. His intellect is as much expanded beyond that of his countrymen, as that of the nineteenth century is in advance of the sixteenth. But his penetration and straight-forward good sense would make him remarkable under any circumstances. With all the impatience of a despotic monarch, exacting the most prompt and implicit obedience to his will, jealous of his authority, and instant to punish, he is yet sagacious, and cautious in altering established customs. His power is founded on popular opinion : his game is to play the people against the chiefs, and he understands it well ; for these fear, and those love him."

During these interviews, in reply to a toast to his health, the King said—"When you drink my health, I am gratified and can thank you ; but when you drink the happiness of my people, I feel as unable adequately to express my feelings as I am incapable of uttering the sound of all their voices."

He then remarked, in reference to toasts, "that the sentiments were not expressed in order that wine might be drunk, but that, under pleasurable excitements, the heart dictated utterance to the mouth."

Captain Moorsom presented him with two Bibles, one English, and the other French, and remarked that the covering of the books was not splendid, but the inside was valuable. To which the King replied, if the books contained what was straight and not crooked, he should be glad to have them; and with regard to the outside, he did not regard a man for the beauty of his countenance, but for the qualities of his heart. The captain then wrote the King's name in one of the Bibles; and it is remarkable that the same book, after being faithfully preserved during the King's life-time, was buried with him amongst other treasures in his splendid tomb.

On leaving Foule Point, Radama took advantage of the kind offer of Captain Moorsom to convey him round the Bay of Antongil. He took with him about two hundred soldiers, while the main body of the troops proceeded by land; and while on board, his mind seemed to be much impressed with the rapidity with which he was conveyed, and the consequent *power* that was imparted. As the vessel sailed out of port, the female singers on land saluted the magnificent object in their usual manner,—Soa, soa, Rabé, mairana. "Beautiful, beautiful! Lightly floating! Large but light! Gone is she, large, and lightly floating!"

During Radama's stay at Foule Point, a French vessel had touched there with communications for him. He, however, refused to see the embassy, or to hold any correspondence with its members, beyond telling them that he was sovereign of the island, and that they were strangers, and had no right to a single foot of the soil. The vessel left the port, threatening vengeance on Radama and his country.

It is stated by Captain Moorsom, that Radama's chief object in visiting Foule Point was to put a final conclusion to an idea long entertained by the French, that they had an equal claim with Radama to the whole of the eastern coast of Madagascar. Monsieur Roux, at that time stationed at St. Mary's, had been active in bringing forward this claim; and in reply to his last communication, the king had sent word to him, that he "would talk about it." "And he now," says Captain Moorsom, "took with him his 13,000 disciplined troops, as a medium of conversation not likely to prove very satisfactory to the other party."

To show the King's idea of discipline, on the return of the troops from an expedition on one occasion, several were charged with having disgraced themselves by cowardice in the field. Under this charge nine were condemned to capital punishment, and suffered the appalling death of being burnt alive.

With the death of the King, the whole aspect of missionary affairs was changed at the capital of Madagascar. Ranavalona, on ascending the throne, gave the missionaries and foreigners residing at the capital, assurances of her intention to govern the kingdom upon the principles adopted by Radama, to carry forward the great plans of education and public improvement which he had commenced, and to continue all the encouragement he had shown them; she had also repeated this on receiving the oath of allegiance of the people; but it soon became evident that these professions were not to be depended on. She was either insincere when she made them, or, what is more probable, the counsellors of another line of policy, those who were in favor of restoring the idolatry of the country had gained the ascendency in the government. These evil counsellors, imagining themselves sufficiently firm in the position they had taken, proceeded, as their first public act, to annul Radama's treaty with the British government. All who were in favor of idolatry and the slave trade, whether natives or foreigners, were of course opposed to this treaty.

Twelve months was the usual period of mourning in Madagascar; but for special reasons the mourning for Radama was caused to cease at the end of ten months. The people then resumed their usual avocations, and preparations were made for the coronation of the Queen. This event was celebrated with the most barbaric pomp and splendor. It was attended by sixty thousand persons, including eight thousand of the military with all their display of uniforms, parade and martial music. The spirit of British discipline, method and order seemed to pervade the whole ceremony. The royal family and all the judges and high officers of the State were present in full estate, and the royal chair or throne shone bright with the royal scarlet and gold. The Queen, having saluted at the tombs of her ancestors the scarlet flags of the idols Manjak-atsiroa and Fantaka—the *idol of the sovereign* and the *idol of the oaths*, was then conducted, in her palanquin, to the sacred stone. Surrounded by five generals, each holding his helmet in one hand and a drawn sword in the other, the band playing the national air, she ascended the stone. Standing there, with her face to the east, she exclaimed—Masina, masina, v'aho—"Am I consecrated, consecrated, consecrated?" The five generals replied—Masina, masina, masina, hianao!—"You are consecrated, consecrated, consecrated!" Then all the crowd shouted—"Trarantitra hianao, Ranavalomanjaka! "Long may you live, Ranavalomanjaka!" The Queen, then descending from the stone on the east side, took the idols Manjakatsiroa and Fantaka into her hands, and addressed them, saying, "My predecessors have given you to me. I put my trust in you; therefore, support me." She then delivered them into the hands of their keepers, entered her palanquin, and was borne to the platform, which she ascended on the east side. She then addressed the immense assembly, and stated, among other things, that she would not change what Radama and her ancestors had done, but that she would add to what they had accomplished.

After the address various tribes came up to acknowledge her sovereignty and assure her of their fidelity. Then followed Arab merchants from Muscat, then the Europeans, and last of all the generals, as representatives of the army. Probably never before had so brilliant a pageant been displayed in Madagascar. The dress of the Queen, on the occasion, is not without interest. On the crown of her head she wore an ornament, resembling a piece of coral, called in French, "*troches*," but in Malagasy "*volahevitra;*" it consisted of five branches, to each of which a red stone, and a small piece of gold, resembling a bell, were attached. The end of the coral was fixed in a round mother-of-pearl shell, placed above the forehead. With this was connected a fine gold chain of native manufacture, which, after being wound several times around the coral, encircled the brow of the Queen, and passed from the forehead over the crown to the back of the head. The Queen wore three necklaces, the first of fine red coral; the second of red stone, ornamented with gold; and the third of red carnelian. Besides these, she wore a scarf, adorned in a curious manner with carnelian stones, called vakantsilchiby. On each arm her Majesty wore three braclets, one of white crystal beads, called vakamiarana; one of oval pearls, ornamented with gold; and the other of fine coral. According to the custom of the country, she also wore anklets of colored glass or precious stones. A white picture, ornamented with gold, was suspended from each of her ear-rings; and on the third and fourth fingers of each hand, she wore rings of gold, ornamented with precious stones, having on the third finger of her right hand a massive gold ring, beautifully polished. Her upper dress was of purple silk, richly ornamented with gold lace, having round the wrists, and on the back, a row of gold buttons. Her lower dress was of white silk; her mantle, or robe, was of superfine scarlet cloth, ornamented similarly to her upper dress; her stockings were white silk, her shoes yellow morrocco, and her forehead was marked with white clay, (tanisave) called, when thus used, "joyful earth." The other members of the royal family were dressed in the European manner.

Reports of an expedition being sent from France against Madagascar, reached the capital in the month of August, 1829, and in fact, six French ships, under the command of Commodore Gourbeyre, arrived in the roads of Tamatavé in the middle of October. Prince Corroller, the officer in command of the station, was taken completely by surprise; the vessels opened their fire on the battery, and in the space of a little more than a quarter of an hour the magazine was blown up, many of the houses were destroyed, great numbers of the people killed, and Corroller with his troops were obliged to retire to Hivondrona, where he remained with a small force, almost destitute of ammunition.

The French followed up the flight, and attacked the prince at

Hivondrona, killed a number of the people, forced them to fly still further into the interior, and then returning pillaged the town; after which, they repaired to their ships, and proceeded northwards towards Foule Point. This was the next port they attacked, but they met with the most determined resistance, and, after losing a considerable number of their men, retired to the Isle of St. Mary's. The French made great efforts, through attempts at negotiation, to establish their claims over the eastern part of the island, but what from the determined resistance of the islanders and the unhealthiness of the climate, they were compelled to leave the coast without effecting any definite results. They sailed from the island in October or November, 1830.

It soon became evident that the regards of the government towards the missionaries were no longer so kindly as they had been under the reign of Radama. A friendly disposition was still manifested towards them, but it seemed to spring rather from a desire to secure the friendship of the English against the French, than from a design to forward the objects of the missionaries. A stimulus to the most vigorous activity in military preparations for the defence of the country, produced by the attack of the French, continued long after they had retired from the coast; and the expectation of its being renewed was accompanied by an equal degree of activity and determination, on the part of the chief officers in the government, to revive superstition and idolatry in the island. The power of the idols was acknowledged as supreme in almost every transaction; public offerings and acts of homage to the idols were multiplied in the capital; and the movements of the government in many of their minute details were regulated by the pretended orders of the Sikidy, or divination, and the use of the tangena was restored with most destructive consequences. In obedience to the orders of the Sikidy, the Queen removed to the village of Ambohimanga, about twenty miles from the capital, where she remained for some months during the early part of 1830. A number of civil and military officers were required to drink poison at the capital; and a general purification of the country, by the same ordeal, was enjoined. Under the latter, many hundreds, if not thousands, of the Malagasy, are supposed to have been sacrificed.

Under such circumstances, the missionaries could not help but consider their stay in the island of very doubtful continuance, and they therefore devoted themselves with renewed efforts towards printing and putting in circulation books of instruction and portions of the Scriptures. A degree of earnestness and attention on the part of the listeners to Sabbath instruction, surpassing any that had before existed, was observed, and a chapel was erected in the northern suburbs of the capital.

The efforts of the artisans were at this time highly prized by the government. Mr. Cameron, who was engaged in the construction of machinery and other public works, had nearly six hundred youths under his charge in constant employment; and while instructing them in the mechanic arts, he encouraged their regular attendance on divine service. On the 29th of May, 1831, twenty of the first converts to Christ in Madagascar, were publicly baptized, in the presence of a highly interested and deeply affected audience. Among these was a former juggler and diviner in the service of the idols, a revealer of destiny, who had made considerable money by the practice of his art. At his baptism he took the name of Paul. These converts gave every evidence of entertaining a thorough appreciation of the Christian religion.

The spirit of that religion, however, is so utterly opposed to idolatry, that there cannot long be a settled state of harmony between them. The Christians began to be hated and despised by the idolaters, as they had been in the earlier days of the church. This opposition on the part of the government soon began to manifest itself in an open, unmistaken manner. Radama, in the earlier part of his reign, had established a law prohibiting the use of wine or spirituous liquors, and though it had never been rigidly executed, especially against the Europeans, it was now taken advantage of by the heathen party to embarass the Christians. It was not allowed to them at the Lord's supper, and the Christians, strangely enough, concluded to celebrate that sacrament by the use of water instead of wine! The persecution was already carried to the extent of prohibiting the scholars at the public schools and the members of the army from receiving the rite of baptism, or joining in the fellowship of the church; and this order was subsequently extended to all other subjects of the Queen. And true to the spirit of slavery, as exhibited not only among barbarians but also in Christian America, the benefits of reading and writing were withheld from every slave in the country.

The government still valued the services of the missionaries, and held a high appreciation of the schools, but it was for their material advantages, and not for the Christianity that they taught. This fact became very evident on the occasion of finishing a canal under the direction of the missionary artisans, between the river Ikiopa and an extensive lake at Amparibé, in the neighborhood of the capital. The lake was made use of as a reservoir of water for mills erected under the superintendence of Mr. Cameron. It was for such uses as these, and for supplying the ranks of the army with intelligent youths, the advantages of which the natives were not slow to perceive, that the schools were encouraged by the government. But the government could no more make use of Christian efforts in this way, than the slave power of the United States could make use of the government for its purposes. The irreconcilable antagonism between sordid self-interest and the purity of Christian principle, the government of Madagascar was wholly unconscious of. Other and more civilized governments are aware of this antagonism, and weakly seek to reconcile it; but the barbarous government of Madagascar did not even suspect its existence.

Again it was reported, in 1831, that the French designed to attack the island, and it was proposed to add 25,000 men, to the forces already enrolled. For this purpose, every one in the schools, both pupils and teachers, upwards of thirteen years of age, was drafted into the army. This proceeding rendered parents averse to sending their children to the public schools, and many of them sent slaves to the schools instead.

Shortly after the report of the arrival of a French expedition at Bourbon, an emissary from the Court of Rome landed at Tamatavé, bearing, as he stated, propositions for introducing the Romish faith among the people. The ecclesiastic represented himself as Count Henry de Solage, vicar apostolic. He had been to India and New South Wales, and stated that he was charged with a special communication from Charles X. of France, and the Pope. He wished to proceed to the capital, but was detained by Prince Carroller on the coast, until the pleasure of the Queen could be known; and letters announcing his arrival were sent up to the capital. In the meantime he persisted in proceeding on his journey, and after advancing a few days, being met by the Queen's officers, his bearers, apprehensive of the consequences of governmental displeasure, left him. He refused to return to the coast, and remained at Ambatoharanana, where, while waiting permission from the Queen to advance, he died suddenly, not without strong suspicions of having poisoned himself.

Anxious to afford any facility for printing the entire Scriptures, and multiplying books, the directors of the London Missionary Society, sent out a new printing press and types; and these the Malagasy government ordered to be taken up to the capital, free of expense to the missionaries. The carrying of packages for the government was often an extremely severe service, and sometimes proved fatal to the bearers. On one occasion several were injured, and two died. When the occurrence was reported to the Queen, she replied, with the heartless indifference of one whose political creed is that the people exist for the sovereign, not the the sovereign for the people— "And what then? Was it not in the service of the government that they died."

The labors of the artisans who taught the natives to work in wood and iron, continued to be highly prized by the people, and Mr. Cameron, who had just finished the erection of a mill, was applied to by the government to undertake the establishment of an iron foundry and a glass manufactory. He acceded to the proposal; and it was arranged that, before commencing the foundry, he should proceed to England, accompanied by two or three native youths, who were not only desirous of visiting that country, but had been selected by the government as eminently qualified to derive great advantage from a visit to the manufactories of Great Britain.

But the divergent tendencies of Christianity and the spirit of idolatry that animated the government, became more manifest every day. The Queen personally did not appear to cherish any unfriendly feeling towards the missionaries, but on the contrary, often seemed disposed to tolerate their exertions; but she was the zealous votary of the idols, on whose favor she was taught to believe her continuance in power depended. Among her ministers were three brothers; the eldest was commander-in-chief of the forces, the second first officer of the palace, and the third a judge; two of them were the Queen's paramours, and all were pledged to raise the idols and former superstitions of the country to their original importance. These brothers exercised in the name of the Queen supreme power in Madagascar; they appear, from the time of Radama's death, to have seized every occasion for impeding the progress of Christianity, and to have aimed at the ultimate expulsion of the missionaries, and the extinction of Christian faith.

Complaints were made against the Christians, such as that they deprived the idols of the land; were always praying; would not swear by the opposite sex; their women were chaste; they observed the Sabbath, which in their total unconsciousness of the excellence of these qualities, remind one of the innocent dullness of the refined Pliny the younger in his report of the Christians to the emperor Trojan.

The Queen at length addressed a communication "to all Europeans, English and French," in which she stated that they might observe the customs of themselves and their ancestors, but that her people must observe the customs of Madagascar. "With regard to religious worship," she said, "whether on the Sunday or not, and the practice of baptism, and the existence of a society, those things cannot be done by my subjects in my country; but with regard to yourselves as Europeans, do that which accords with the customs of your ancestors, and your own customs. But if there be knowledge of the arts and sciences, that will be beneficial to my subjects in the country, teach that, for it is good; therefore I tell you of this, my friends and relations, that you may hear of it. (Saith) Ranavalomanjaka."

To this a reply was returned by six missionaries, manifesting regret at the Queen's determination, and requesting that the teaching of the word of God, together with the arts and sciences, might not be suppressed.

At length the Queen's determination was announced to an assembly of 150,000 persons, including 15,000 troops under arms. The following extract from a long edict addressed to the people in that occasion will serve to show the tenor of the whole:—"As to baptism, societies, places of worship, distinct from the schools, and the observance of the Sabbath, how many rulers are there in this land? Is it not I alone that rule? These things are not to be done, they are unlawful in my country, saith Ranavalomanjaka; for they are not the customs of our ancestors, and I do not change their customs, excepting as to things alone which improve my country."

She denounced death against all her native subjects who disobeyed this edict. The name of Jesus was not to be invoked except in connexion with the national idols, the sun, moon, etc. The Queen was undoubtedly encouraged to this course, in part, by the expectation of receiving instruction in the manufacture of muskets, and in other arts, from some natives of France, who engaged to teach all that the English had taught, without associating with it any religious instruction; and partly to a fear of becoming dependent on the British government, of whose enroachments in India, Ceylon, and South Africa she had received very highly colored accounts. The government had indeed always manifested extreme jealousy of foreigners residing in the island, and a fear of all foreign intercourse with the country.

Deprived of much of their means of usefulness among the people, the missionaries directed all their energies to the completion of the holy Scriptures. Assisted by native youths, they also completed a Dictionary of the English and Malagasy languages, to which a second part of Malagasy and English was added. But as the spirit of the government naturally became more and more hostile, the missionaries were compelled gradually to withdraw, until finally the last of their number left the capital, with deep regret, in the month of July, 1836, eighteen years after their first arrival in the country.

Fresh idols were now continually brought to the capital; new altars were erected in several places; tombs, altars, and other objects of superstitious veneration, that had been lying in ruins, were repaired; new ceremonies were appointed, and offerings more frequently presented. In all these attempts to restore the influence of idolatry, the Queen seemed to take the lead, being at times occupied for several days together in the observance of idolatrous ceremonies, and inaccessible to any excepting those who were engaged in the service of the idols.

In the early part of 1837, great scarcity prevailed in many parts of the country, and multitudes, it was feared, died from want. The sufferings of the people induced no relaxation of the oppression and severity of the government. Between the departure of the last of the missionaries in 1836, and the month of March, 1837, nine hundred criminals, charged with various offences, were put to death, having been declared guilty by the tangena; fifty-six were burnt to death, and sixty killed by spearing and other means, making a fearful total of 1,016 executions in the short space of eight months. That the country under these circumstances should prosper, was impossible; and it is not surprising that agriculture was neglected, and that multitudes driven by despair had recourse to violence and plunder; universal anarchy and complete desolation was only prevented by the military forces of the government.

In the year 1836, the Queen determined on sending an embassy to England and France. It is probable that reverses which the army had met with in the southern part of the island, the favor shown by English vessels to those which her army had attacked, and the fear that some chief, thus aided, might wrest the government from her hands, led the Queen to the adoption of this measure.

The embassy, consisting of six officers, left Madagascar in the summer of 1836. The French ship Mathilde, Captain Garnot, was chartered by the Queen to take them from Tamatavé to England and France, and back to Madagascar. The embassy arrived at Port Louis, in Mauritius, early in October. They were courteously received by his Excellency Sir William Nicolay, the Governor; and, after a short delay, proceeded to the Cape of Good Hope, where respectful attentions were also paid them by the Governor, Sir B. D'Urban.

Leaving the Cape, the embassy proceeded to Havre de Grace, and from there were conducted, by Captain Garnot, in a steam packet to London, where they arrived in February, and took up their lodgings at Radley's hotel.

After an interview with Lord Palmerston, Secretary of State for foreign affairs, they were presented to the King at St. James on the first of March.

During their stay in London they visited several national establishments, and some of the principal manufactories. In company with some of their old acquaintances, the missionaries, they visited the Bank, the Mint, the Tower, the London Docks, Woolwich Arsenal, and Dockyard, the Thames Tunnel, St. Paul's, the Museum, the Monument, Galley of Practical Science, Apollonicon, Colosseum, Zoölogical Gardens, London Gas-works, the British and Foreign School, Borough Road, the National and the Infant Schools, Baldwin's Gardens, etc., etc. They were also much gratified by the inspection of the paper manufactory of Messrs. Pewtress & Co., the Iron Foundry of Messrs. Maudsley & Co., the Pottery of Mr. Green, at Lambeth, and the Glass-works of Mr. Pellatt, at Bankside.

On Monday, the 6th of March, they attended a meeting of the Directors of the London Missionary Society, at the Mission House, to which they had been invited. They were received with kindness and respect; and to the address of the Directors they made a brief but appropriate reply.

On the 7th of March they had an audience of the King at Windsor. On this occasion the Rev. Mr. Freeman presented the King a copy of the holy Scriptures in the Malagasy language, which had been printed at the Mission press in Madagascar. The King received the Bible in a manner that could not fail to impress the embassy with a deep sense of the high regard entertained by the British Sovereign for this volume of divine revelation, and the satisfactory result of missionary effort its existence in the Malagasy language afforded.

During the interview, his Majesty graciously introduced the embassy to the Queen, who addressed them with great courtesy and kindness. Afterwards, while passing through the appartments of the castle, they again met her Majesty, who again entered into conversation with them. Having learned that, although many of the Malagasy had been instructed by the missionaries, yet, in consequence of an edict of the Queen of Madagascar, no native could profess Christianity, her Majesty said to them, "Tell the Queen of Madagascar from me, that she can do nothing so beneficial for her country as to receive the Christian religion."

On the 19th of March, 1837, having had their final interview with the government, and received a written communication for their sovereign, the embassy sailed for Calais, on their way to Paris. After concluding negotiations with the French government, they embarked for Madagascar, and arrived at Tamatavé in the month of September following. Thence they proceeded to the capital.

About the time that the embassy returned from Europe, the forces of the Malagasy government returned from an unsuccessful expedition against Adriansolo, Chief of the Sakalavas, in which they had been utterly defeated and put to rout. The government, however, was in no way disheartened by it, and proceeded to fit out another expedition. The same jealousy of European influence continued to be exhibited. Captain Garnot, who had conveyed the embassy to Europe, repaired to the capital, on his return, charged with proposals, it is said, from the French government, to enter into commercial and other relations with the government. These, it is reported, were refused by the Queen, who closed her transactions with the French captain, paying him in dollars for the expenses incurred on account of the embassy, and declined any mercantile dealings with himself, or those whom he was deputed to represent.

The last of the missionaries, as we have already stated, left the island in 1836, eighteen years after they had commenced their labors there. But from the island of Mauritius they still watched for an opportunity to return. Mr. Johns visited

Tamatavé in July, 1837, and though he found the door shut against farther missionary effort, he was pleased to find that the native Christians still continued in the faith and purity of the Gospel, shining as lights in the midst of a perverse and benighted generation. Though repeatedly annoyed by the government, they were accustomed to read the Scriptures at the hour of midnight in their own houses, or other places of concealment, and to meet in small companies for singing and prayer. They were closely watched by the government, though no infringement of the edict of the Queen was discovered until about the first Sabbath of August, 1837, when a number of them were discovered on a mountain, not far from the capital, engaged in religious exercises. Among these was a woman by the name of Rafararavy, on whose premises some Bibles and other Christian publications were discovered. She was apprehended and imprisoned, her home given up to plunder, and her hands and feet manacled with irons. She was menaced in vain during a period of from eight to ten days, to induce her to impeach her companions. She remained firm and perfectly composed, and was put to death by spearing on the 14th of August, 1837, thus suffering a martyrdom as pure, simple, and unmixed with alloy as any that have characterized the earliest ages of the church.

Thus gloomily falls the curtain over the first act of protestant missionary labors in the Island of Madagascar. Nor was it to rise again until after the lapse of a dreary period of some eighteen years more, during which time the people were subject to a reign of idolatry, wretchedness, and blood.

Executions, poisonings, reduction to slavery, plunderings, and other punishments, bad as they were, did not complete the catalogue of the people's woes. In devising plans of cruelty and malignity, Queen * Ranavalona seemed highly gifted. For instance, in the year 1845 it is known that she made a progress to the province of Mancrincrina, ostensibly, to enjoy the sport of buffalo-hunting, and that she was accompanied by more than 50,000 persons. All the officers and nobles, far and near, in and around Tananarivo, were invited to attend, and that the procession might appear as magnificent as possible, every one had to bring with him all his servants and slaves. Ten thousand soldiers accompanied

---

* Ranavalonamanjaka means Queen Ranavalona, manjaka signifying, like the Hebrew *Melek*, King, or Chief, and with the feminine termination, Queen.

them, and nearly as many more bearers, and 12,000 men were kept a day's journey in advance, to repair the roads and make them wider. The inhabitants of the villages through which the Queen passed were forced to furnish a number of men to go forward and prepare the night's lodging for the royal family, which had to be surrounded with intrenchments against possible attacks from enemies. As she made no provision except for her own support, all her followers, under the most disadvantageous circumstances, were obliged to provide for themselves. This was an exceedingly difficult task to perform, for even the majority of the nobles had to suffer the greatest privations; for, wherever a little rice was left, it was sold at such a high price that only the richest were able to purchase it. In consequence, it is supposed that during the four months of the progress 10,000 persons, including women and children, died from starvation.

Previous to this, in 1837, the Queen, having received a report from her ministers that there were many magicians, thieves, violators of graves, and other evil-doers among the people, convened a Kabary on the occasion, and proclaimed that all who delivered themselves up should have their lives spared to them, but all who failed should suffer the punishment of death. Nearly sixteen hundred men gave themselves up accordingly. Of these, ninety-six were denounced; and of these, fourteen were burnt alive, some were thrown from the rock, others were put into holes and had scalding water thrown upon them, others again were speared or poisoned, some were beheaded, and some few had their limbs cut off. But the most barbarous punishment of all was to sew up victims in sacks, with only their heads protruding, and thus leaving them to die and rot. Yet, in total disregard of the word given by the government, those who had been their own accusers, suffered a worse fate, if possible, than all the rest. Fastened together in gangs of four or five, with heavy irons around their necks and wrists, they were permitted to go free, only being watched by guards to see that their irons were not filed off. When one of the group died, his head was cut off in order to free him from the rest of the gang, leaving his irons to weigh upon the others, until finally the whole group perished.

It is needless, however, to dwell upon the practices of barbarism in the absence of Christianity. We give these darker shades of human nature merely to add another to the numerous proofs which we already have, of the great blessings which a Christian people enjoy, and of the source from which those blessings are derived.

In 1853 the condition of Madagascar was such as to induce the London Missionary Society to send out agents to see if the missionary work of former years could be resumed there. The Rev. Mr. Ellis, from whose excellent writings the most of this account has been taken, and Mr. Cameron were the agents chosen, and they arrived at Tamatavé in July of that year. They found that the state of sentiment in the country had assumed a distinct party shape, and that while the government and its supporters were decidedly in favor of maintaining the idols, the Sikidy, tangena, slavery, coerced labor, and all the other customs of their ancestors, there was another party which was equally decided in favor of learning, of having the schools reopened, and of Christian improvement generally. Though many Christians had been put to death, driven into exile or reduced to bonds and degradation, yet there were found to be at least one thousand persons, in the capital and its vicinity, who were known to each other and mutually recognized as disciples of Christ. Many of them were even holding offices of great responsibility, chiefly, if not solely, in consequence of their ability, integrity, and known worth. It was supposed that the Christianity of some of them was known and connived at, on account of the value of their services to the government.

The heir apparent at that time, the son of the Queen, was a man of gentle manners and amiable disposition, and both he and his wife were supposed to be members of the church, and devoted friends of its persecuted and afflicted flock. His manners were described to be more like those of an English gentleman than of a Malagasy. Prince Rakodond–Radama, or Prince Rakoto, as he was more commonly called, was then about twenty-three years of age, and he was marked as being unlike any tribe of the islanders, resembling rather the Moldavian-Greek than the Malay, or the African race. His features wore an expression of child-like goodness, and he was beloved by the people, and especially by his mother. Yet he had bitter enemies among the supporters of idol-worship, the chief of whom was a nephew of the Queen, and his rival to the throne. He was kind-hearted, as averse to the shedding of blood as his mother was prone to it, often interfered to obtain a reversal of the sentences of death, showed a fondness for the society of

Europeans, and often wore their dress. Yet, behind all this, one might have perceived an ambition for the government, but without that energy, firmness and ability which would be necessary to render his reign safe to any great interest that might be involved in it.

His rival, the leader of the anti-Christian party was represented to be a shrewd, ambitious, daring man, with considerable business talent and large property. No efforts were spared by him and his party, it was said, to prevent the accession of Prince Rakoto to the throne. He was represented to the Queen as totally unacquainted with the business of government, and bewitched by the Christians, and that to place the sovereignty in his hands would be to promote dissatisfaction, and to sacrifice the good of the Kingdom. And this was probably the Queen's own opinion, for she believed that the Christians had taken advantage of his amiable temper and inexperience to draw him over to their party, and this had excited her extreme indignation.

It was concluded by the missionary agents that the way for recommencing the labors of the Society in Madagascar was not yet fully open, but that the time for that event was approaching they had no doubt. In the following summer (1854) Mr. Ellis visited the island again, and he found the greatest eagerness on the part of the Christians to have copies of the sacred writings. One man assured him that for many years he had spent his time in transcribing portions of God's word for those of his brethren who were destitute of it, the Bible having been destroyed, as far as possible, by the agents of the government. The feeling in favor of Christianity and education was discovered to be more extensive than had been supposed, and persons who were little suspected of a leaning to Christianity, were found to be either in the possession of Christian books, or eager to obtain them. A strong conviction of the value of education was prevalent among the middle and upper classes. The chiefs and officers who were able to read and write, taught their own sons, and deemed such a knowledge essential to their holding any place under government, or making their way in the world. As an evidence of the hold which Christian faith had taken upon the minds of the people, Mr. Ellis referred to the letters, which, of their own free motion, some of the Malagasy Christians forwarded to their "beloved brethren in London." In their matter and spirit these letters resembled not a little the epistles of the New Testament.

CHAPTER V.

We have thus far followed such glimpses of the history of Madagascar as the operations of the English and their missionaries furnish us, with occasional references to the long and persistent efforts which the French have from time to time made in that quarter; and we come now to speak of an attempt to improve the condition of the government of the island and of the people which appears to be wholly French, both in its design and execution. The object in view, in making this attempt, would appear to be of the most philanthropic kind, but the peculiar mode of effecting it, was more suited to the brilliant genius of the French than to the slower and surer course of action which characterizes the English. In short, a French gentleman by the name of Lambert sought to accomplish by a brilliant, diplomatic feat, by one single *coup d'état*, as much as the English had done by long and toilsome years of patient missionary effort. His combinations were of the most approved kind, according to the ideas of those who proceed in this way to carry out their benevolent designs, and the actors in the diplomatic charade were all skillfully chosen, and artistically assigned and arranged to their respective parts. The usual simulated antagonism between the parties, some being in favor and some against, some coarse, brutal and offensive in their manners, and some polite, smiling and kindly, in which the secret societies of France are such adepts, was not forgotten, together with the skillfully manufactured false rumors which are conceived so necessary by those societies to attain a good end. These characters were Mr. Lambert himself, the celebrated Madame Pfeiffer, the great traveler, Mr. Latrobe, a French gentleman, residing at the capital of Madagascar, Madamoiselle Julie and her two brothers, Prince Rokoto, Mr. Marius, and severel French missionaries, who, in half disguise to escape persecutions from the Queen, were residing in the island.

Mr. Lambert was a large sugar-planter, in the Island of Mauritius, having under his control some six hundred laborers and two thousand acres of land, which produced from two to three millions pounds of sugar annually. Though like the planters of the Mauritius and Island of Bourbon generally, receiving the beef and rice for his laborers from Madagascar, he never visited that island until 1855. Seeing the wanton wretchedness and misery which the Queen inflicted upon her people, a generous wish arose within his breast to free them from her tyrannical control. He easily gained the friendship of the amiable Prince Rakoto, who declared that he cared not who ruled over the island so long as the government was good and just, and they soon came to an understanding, and entered into treaty stipulations, Mr. Lambert intending to seek assistance from either the French or English government.

Accordingly, in the year 1856, he went to Paris, and in a private interview with the Emperor, laid open the boundless misery to which the people of Madagascar were exposed from their government, and appealed to him for help in their behalf. Failing to elicit the sympathy of the Emperor in a philanthropic object, which might not fully accord with the political interests of France, Mr. Lambert proceeded to England, and laid the matter before the English Minister, Lord Clarendon. But instead of deriving aid from this quarter, he imagined that obstacles were thrown in his way by the London Missionary Society, who feared, it is said, that in the event of the French occupation of the island, the Roman religion might be the only form of worship introduced and licensed, which, in their opinion, would be a much greater misfortune for the inhabitants than even the cruel sway of Ranavalona herself. It is even charged that the Society determined to oppose Mr. Lambert's designs, and sent an especial missionary for this purpose to Tananarivo, to acquaint the Queen of what his designs were.

On Mr. Lambert's return to the Mauritius in November, 1856, he stopped at Cape Town, South Africa, where he met, as if by accident, with Madame Pfeiffer. In her extensive travels over the globe she had long entertained an ardent desire to visit the Island of Madagascar. A native of Vienna, the capital of Austria, she had now attained the age of sixty years, and was on her second voyage to the Dutch East India possessions. On arriving at Cape Town, Mr. Lambert went on board her ship, introduced himself to her, said that he had heard while in Paris of her intention to visit Madagascar, and invited her to accompany him to that island. He had written to the Queen, from Paris, he said, for permission to land in the island, for no one was permitted to land there without her approval, and he had no doubt but that he could gain permission for the landing of Madame Pfeiffer also. But in consequence of the rainy season, the voyage there could not be undertaken till the following April. In the meantime, however, she could spend the interval at his house in the Mauritius.

With equal surprise and delight Madame Pfeiffer accepted this invitation. Though Sir George Gray, the Governor of the Cape, offered to accompany her on a journey through the territory if she would stay, yet nothing could induce her to give up the prospect of a visit to Madagascar. At the Mauritius she was warned against Mr. Lambert as a very dangerous man; but whether she suspected any of his designs or not, she was determined to accompany him on his journey to Tananarivo.

At length on the 25th of April, 1857, Madame Pfeiffer embarked on board an old Trafalgar battle-ship, then a cattle transport from Madagascar to Mauritius, for Tamatavé, where she was joined by Mr. Lambert on the 13th of May. Previous to sailing for Madagascar, Mr. Lambert visited Zanzibar and Mozambique on behalf of the French Government, for the purpose of *hiring* negro laborers for the Island of Bourborn. This was a new species of slave-trade, invented by the French and acquiesced in by the English. The negro was designed to be in servitude only five years, and was to receive two dollars per month from his master besides board and lodging. After his five years had expired, he might find his way back to Africa if he had saved money enough to pay his passage, which, however, one can readily conceive there might be many obstacles and opposing interests to prevent; for the interests of planters are hardly more in accordance with the purer motives of philanthropy than are the politics of States.

At Tamatavé, while waiting for Mr. Lambert, Madame Pfeiffer became the guest successively of Madamoiselle Julie to whom Mr. Lambert had given her a letter, and of her two brothers who had estates in the vicinity. These persons had received a French education either in Bourbon or Paris, and yet they preferred to lapse into barbarism instead of living up to the standard of civilization. Madamoiselle Julie kept a harbor boarding-house; and at times there were as many as five vessels in the harbor.

At length, the journey for the capital was commenced on the 19th of May. The party consisted of Mr. Marius, Mr. Lambert and Madame Pfeiffer. Mr. Marius was a Frenchman, who had resided on the island twenty years. He undertook the office of interpreter and the general direction of the journey. It required four hundred men to bear the presents which Mr. Lambert had provided, from his own purse, at a cost of

nearly forty thousand dollars, for the Queen and Prince Rakoto. These presents consisted of rich Parisian dresses for the
Queen and Princesses of her family, a splendid uniform, em-
broidered with gold, for the Prince, valuable objects of art of
all kinds, including musical clocks, barrel organs, etc. The
carriers of these presents received nothing for their services,
such labor in Madagascar being compulsory. Besides these
carriers there were two hundred for the travelers and their
own personal baggage, who were paid by Mr. Lambert. For
the whole distance of two hundred miles from Tamatavé to
Tananarivo, each bearer is usually allowed only one dollar
without food; but in this case they were delighted in receiving rations besides their pay.

The objects along the route were new and full of interest to
Madame Pfeiffer, and everything went on smoothly and pleas-
antly, the journey seeming like a triumphal procession during
the latter part of the way. Among the curious objects that
arrested the attention, was the multiplicity of lightning rods
that were seen, every large house seeming to be provided with
one. These had been introduced by Mr. Latrobe, as a protec
tion against the peculiarly violent thunder-storms that prevail
in that region. As many as three hundred persons were killed
annually, it was said, in Tananarivo alone, by lightning
though this is doubtless a great exaggeration. On drawing
near the capital the procession was met by a young son of
Prince Rakoto five years old, whom Mr. Lambert had adopted
as his own at his previous visit, also by adherents of the Prince
officers of high rank, a corps of singing girls, and throngs of
curious people. A band of music that had been sent out for
the purpose led the van, while a crowd of soldiers and citizens
followed up the rear. At length, after several delays, occasioned
by awaiting the Queen's final determination, which was never
arrived at until the Sikidy had been carefully consulted, the
party entered the gates of the city, and proceeded to the house
of Mr. Latrobe.

This gentleman was born in France, and was the son of a
saddler. He had served awhile in the cavalry, but after his
father's death, growing sick of the service, and having a rov
ing disposition, he procured a substitute, and embarked for
the East Indies. In Bombay he established several work
shops, repaired steam engines, manufactured weapons and
saddlery, and did a good business. But owing to a restless
spirit, he gave up his workshops to a friend, and in 1831 or

barked for the Indian Archipelago. The ship, driven out of her course by a storm, was wrecked on the Island of Madagascar, and he not only lost all he possessed, but was reduced to slavery and taken to the capital to be sold. His skill in manufacturing weapons and other articles coming to the knowledge of the Queen, she entered into an agreement with him to give him his liberty if he would serve her faithfully for five years. Establishing a workshop, he furnished the Queen with all kinds of weapons, powder, and even small cannons, and so highly did she esteem his opinions that she consulted him in several important affairs, yielding not unfrequently to his appeals in behalf of those who had been sentenced to death. And not only was he favored by the Queen, but he became very popular with the nobles and people, to whom he acted as physician, confidential friend and helper. The five years passed away, and as he had received from his patroness house, home, and slaves, and had married a native woman, by whom he had a son, he gradually became radicated to the soil. Though free to go, yet he chose to stay, and in course of time he established other work-shops for glass-blowing, indigo dyeing, soap and tallow boiling, and a distillery for rum. He also strove to introduce European fruits into the island, though his example in this respect was not readily followed by the natives.

At Mr. Latrobe's house the travelers were introduced to two clergymen, Europeans, who, though missionaries, feared to have the fact known, and in consequence were for the time being under the protecting roof of their friend, one as a physician, and the other as a tutor to Mr. Latrobe's son, who had returned from Paris, where he had been sent to be educated. Mr. Latrobe's style of living was sumptuous in the extreme, his table being loaded with luxuries served on massive silver, and his champagne being drunk from silver goblets, a style which he had introduced himself for economy's sake to save china ware, and in which he had been initiated by the nobles. While the travelers were at dinner, and the champagne was being handed round, a slave came running in to announce Prince Rakoto. In a moment afterwards the Prince himself entered and rushed into Mr. Lambert's arms, and the two remained for a long time in each other's embrace, without finding words to express their joy.

Thus far everything had gone on brilliantly and to the satisfaction of the parties concerned. Nor were flattering appearances destined to end yet. Mr. Lambert and his lady compan-

ion had the honor of being introduced at Court; Madame Pfeiffer
was invited to play the piano before the Queen; a splendid
fancy ball was got up among the nobles, excelling in some
respects the flare and gayety of Paris itself, and, to crown all,
Mr. Lambert and Madame Pfeiffer were urged by the Queen to
dance together a *pas de deux* at Court! This reasonable wish
of the Queen was announced to the astonished couple by Prince
Rakoto in person, and when we consider the work in which
they were engaged it seemed rather like a bitter sarcasm than
as the mere curiosity of a simpled-minded barbarian. Sickness
was pleaded as an excuse for not complying with this request,
Mr. Lambert suffering from the fever.

At length, on the 6th of June, a grand dinner was given in
honor of Prince Rakoto by Mr. Latrobe in his garden-house.
The dinner-party was bright and cheerful, and Mr. Lambert
was in the highest spirits. The feast was followed by music
and dancing until ten o'clock at night, when, at the request of
Mr. Lambert, Madame Pfeiffer broke up the party, alleging the
effects of a previous indisposition for so doing. Favored by a
bright moonlight, the party marched away from the summer-
house to the strains of merry music, in a manner calculated to
lull all suspicions as to the covert conspiracy that was going
on under this fair exterior. The party being dismissed, Prince
Rakoto and Mr. Lambert called Madame Pfeiffer into a side
room of Mr. Latrobe's dwelling house; and the Prince assured
her for a second time that the private contract between Mr.
Lambert and himself had been drawn up with his entire con-
currence, and that it was a gross calumny that he was intoxi-
cated when he signed it. He said that Mr. Lambert had come
to Madagascar by his wish, and with the intention, in conjunc-
tion with himself and a portion of the nobility and soldiers, to
remove Queen Ranavalona from the throne, but without
depriving her of freedom, her wealth, or the honors which
were her due.

Mr. Lambert, on his part, informed her that the dinner had
been given at Mr. Latrobe's garden-house because everything
could be more quietly discussed there; that she had been
requested to break up the party in order that it might appear
to have been given in her honor, and finally, that they had
gone through town with noisy music in order that the object
might appear to be mere social entertainment. She was then
shown in the house a complete little arsenal of guns, sabres,
daggers, pistols, and leather shirts of mail for arming the

conspirators, and informed that every preparation had been made, and that the time of action might be looked for every hour.

The decisive day, however, was not fixed upon until the 20th of June, when the following plan was to be carried into execution. The Prince was to dine at eight o'clock in the evening with Mr. Lambert, Marius, Latrobe and his son, in the garden-house belonging to the latter, and to that point all the reports from the other conspirators were to be carried, in order that it might be known how every thing was progressing, and whether every man was at his post. After the dinner, at eleven o'clock at night, the gentlemen were to march home to the upper part of the town, accompanied by music, as if returning from a feast; and every man was then to remain quiet in his own house until two o'clock. At that hour, all the conspirators were to steal silently into the palace, the gates of which Prince Raharo, the Chief of the army, was to keep open, and guarded by officers devoted to Prince Rakoto; they were to assemble in the great court-yard, in front of the Queen's appartments, and at a given signal loudly to proclaim Prince Rakoto King! The new ministers, who had already been nominated by the Prince, were to explain to the Queen that this was the will of the nobles, the military, and the people; and, at the same time, the thunder of cannon from the royal palace was to announce to the people the change in the government, and deliverance from the sanguinary rule of Queen Ranavalona!

But unluckily, this bright scheme was not carried out. The combination did not work. While the chief conspirators were still at table, they received from Prince Raharo the disastrous news that, from unforseen obstacles, he had found it impossible to fill the palace exclusively with officers in the Prince's interest, that he could not consequently keep the gates open that night, and that the attempt must be deferred to some more favorable opportunity. In vain did the Prince send messenger after messenger to him. He could not be induced to risk an attempt; and the plan wholly failed.

Prince Rakoto had headed a similar conspiracy in 1856; the hour had been fixed on, but everything miscarried through the apparent sudden defection of the commander-in-chief of the army. It was suspected that this one of the principal actors in the scheme was in fact false to his engagements, that he was faithful to the Queen, and at heart a partisan of Prince Ramboasalama, the cousin and rival of Prince Rakoto, and whom, previous to the birth of Rakoto, the Queen had declared her heir and successor.

It was on the day succeeding this failure of Mr. Lambert's diplomatic arrangements that he and his lady friend received an invitation to dance the *pas de deux* at the palace—certainly a provoking conclusion to such a brilliant and promising beginning!

But if the affair had ended here, it would have been well. Unfortunately the reaction fell in redoubled force upon the native Christians. A great Kabary was called by the Queen for the purpose of hunting out and punishing with death all who remained true to their Christian belief. A considerable number were discovered and put to the most insufferable torture. One old woman was dragged into the market-place, and had her backbone sawn asunder. The Europeans were confined in their own quarters, and kept in a constant state of apprehension as to their fate. One consideration alone seemed to operate in their behalf; and that was that in case they should be put to death, the European governments might exact from the government of Madagascar a terrible retribution.

In the midst of the Queen's disfavor, however, she sent to Mr. Lambert for the presents which he had brought, and they were sent up to the palace. But they were presently returned, and Mr. Lambert, Mr. Marius, the two other Europeans, and Madame Pfeiffer were ordered to depart from the city within an hour. Mr. Latrobe was allowed to remain twenty-four hours longer, and to carry off all his movable property except slaves. His son might choose either to go or stay, just as he pleased. They were allowed carriers for themselves and property (including the presents), and a military escort was assigned to them, which appeared to execute its orders to the very letter, if we can judge by the inconvenience to which they put the party. The journey from the capital to Tamatavé is usually performed in eight days; but on this occasion the party were detained on the route fifty-three days, and at times in low, swampy places, as if the design was that they should die from the fever. At last, however, after suffering every conceivable hardship, embittered by indignities of the most disgraceful character, the party arrived at Tamatavé, and the Commandant of the military escort saw them on board of a vessel bound for the Mauritius, where they arrived on the 22d of September.

When leaving Tananarivo, and while passing through the market-place, they saw, as a parting scene, and as a horrid comment on their benevolent efforts, ten Christians who were being tormented and killed.

Madame Pfeiffer asserts that the London Missionary Society had sent a chosen member to forewarn the Queen of Mr. Lambert's designs, to assure her that the English government desired ardently to continue the same friendly relations with her country which had existed in the time of George IV., represented Mr. Lambert as a spy in the employment of the French government, and predicted that he would speedily make his appearance, accompanied by a body of French troops, to depose her in favor of her son: that the missionary read a long lecture to Prince Rakoto on the exceeding turpitude of his conduct in meditating a revolt against his royal mother, declaring that the English government had been so shocked by the news as to *put on mourning*: that the Prince consented to excuse himself, by asserting in reply that had he indeed intended such an act he would have merited reproach; but that such was not the case, as he merely wished to deprive the Queen of the power of perpetrating cruelties, every other privilege being retained by her, and as for himself he asked nothing at all: that the missionary had boasted everywhere that he had been invited to Madagascar by the Queen, and that he had been favorably received by her and the Prince, while the facts in the case were that after a short stay at the capital of four weeks, he was ordered to leave, against his remonstrances on account of the unhealthiness of the season, the Queen being highly exasperated against him for distributing Bibles, and the Prince resenting his behavior toward Mr. Lambert.

We mention these charges merely to show more clearly to the mind of the reader the great temptations to which missionaries are often exposed, to interfere with political matters, and thus to overlook the first great principle of their Divine Master, who rejected the offered control of all the Kingdoms of the world. If there has been any one thing that operated more than another to destroy the usefulness of the Romish missionaries in their long labors in the East, a field that has been open to them more than three hundred years, and in which their success in spreading the Gospel has amounted to little, or nothing, it is a neglect of this vital principle, and an exhibition, on the other hand, of a great aptness to proceed at once to meddle with the political relations of the countries which they visit. True religion possesses a moral dignity that rejects the suggestions of mere political cunning the moment that they are offered; and the missionary can seldom or never attain to any desirable end unless this dignity distinguishes every trait of his daily walk and ministration.

Another night of heathen superstition and darkness settles upon the Island of Madagascar, in which idolatry and persecution prevail like feverish dreams. But this state of things was not destined to a long continuance. Queen Ranavalona was already advanced in years, being some seventy years or more in age, and her death therefore was an event that might be expected to occur at any moment. It took place, in fact, in 1861.

Prince Rokoto ascended the throne as Radama II.; and he immediately sent a message to the Governor of the Mauritius inviting free intercourse, stating that he had proclaimed commercial liberty throughout his territory, with equitable customs regulations at all the ports; that he had intimated that he was not disposed to accept the protection of France or of any other power, and to have appointed an Englishman, long a faithful adherent, as his Prime Minister; that he had also declared his preference for protestant Christianity, and had written letters to protestant missionaries at the Mauritius and the Cape, informing them that the land is once more open to the preachers of the Gospel.

As might be expected, Mr. Lambert and Pere Jouan who was one of the priests in disguise at the capital of Madagascar at the time of Mr. Lambert's diplomatic visit there, made haste to pay their respects in person to the new sovereign. They were shortly followed by two Romish priests; and it became manifest that it was their design to make Romanism the prevailing religion of the island. The newspaper press in the Island of Bourbon boldly asserted the right of France to the supreme political power in Madagascar, and to the submission of that island as a dependency of the Imperial government. The press of Paris assumed the same ground; and on the doors of Romish churches in Cork, Ireland, were posted the following notice:—*Young men wanted for Missionaries to Madagascar.*

An embassy was sent to the island by the Governor of the Mauritius to present the congratulations of the English Government to Radama on his ascension to the throne; and the English Government prepared to maintain the independence of the new sovereign. The directors of the London Missionary Society at once took measures to resume its labors in that island, using, for this purpose, funds that had been especially donated many years before, and which had not been diverted to any other object. Mr. Ellis embarked again for Madagascar in November, 1861, having concluded arrangements by which he was to be followed in a short time by a corps of six missionaries.

The Christians who had endured so long a persecution and were still alive, now came forth from their hiding places, from prison and places of torture, and the people were astonished to see what a considerable number had escaped with their lives. Subsequent events showed that there must have been some 7,000 Christians in the island. Some of them could not walk, from the enfeeblement occasioned by the heavy fetters with which their limbs had been loaded. The King told them to write to their friends in London, and to tell them that King Radama II. reigned, and that whoever wishes to come up can come.

Mr. Ellis arrived at Tananarivo about the middle of June, 1862, and was received with great cordiality by the King, officers of the government, and pastors and members of churches. Thirty miles from the capital he was met by a large number of Christians from there. As the two parties approached each other, the party from the capital commenced singing praises to God, in which the party with Mr. Ellis joined until they met and halted. The welcome extended to the English missionaries was of the warmest and most impressive kind. Hundreds crowded their doors continually, and thronged the churches on the Sabbath from an early hour in the morning till late in the afternoon.

Romish priests and sisters of mercy were present at the capital urging their peculiar views upon the people; but the preference for the protestant ideas, books, and modes of worship was evident and decided. The King gave assurance of perfect liberty of conscience to every one to worship as he pleased. He opened the prison doors and set the Christian captive free. He dispatched messengers to recall the remnant of the condemned ones from remote and pestilential districts, to which they had been banished, and where numbers had died from disease and exhaustion, occasioned by the rude and heavy bars of iron with which they had been chained, neck and neck together. He sent to remote and hostile tribes presents and messages which made them his fast friends; and he abolished the tangena, sikidy, and other idolatrous usages.

But the King, who had been so forward to assume the cares and responsibilities of the government, was little aware of the troubles that were in store for him. The conflicting interests of Paganism, Protestantism and Romanism, which now centered upon the capital, and, it may be said, upon the head of the State himself, were enough to disconcert a wiser and more experienced man than he. If amidst the perplexities thus occasioned he should become disconcerted, inconsistent and confused, and should even take to drink, as a counter excitement to the annoyances which he met with in the administration of the government, it is no more than we have frequently seen in the United States on the part of men who have been ranked among our ablest and best of statesmen. The character of the King, in the course of a few months, seemed to undergo a change. But though distinguished for amiable qualities and an instinctive hatred of cruelty, he had never become a Christian. An impulsive and excitable temperament exposed him to certain evil influences thrown around him; and while naturally inclined to superstition, and when under the influence of strong drink, he behaved, at times, it is said, like a madman. Without the ability or experience to meet the requirements of the new condition of things, he became a time-server, siding at one time with the Pagans, at another with the Romanists, and at another with the Protestants, and thus endeavored by exciting the jealousies and self-interests of the various parties, to keep the power in his own hands. He was a fit subject to be acted on by crafty and designing men; and unfortunately the temptation to act upon him was only too great. The consequences to the King proved disastrous. He was assassinated on the 12th of May, 1863, in his palace, by a party of nobles led by his Prime Minister.

In the course of the contest between the King and his nobles, he had claimed that he alone was sovereign, and that his word alone was law; and that his person was sacred, and that he would punish severely the oppressors of his will, an idea of kingly authority natural to all those who exercise it, but which the people of the Western world have succeeded in reducing to some limitations. It was natural, too, that the King should strive to maintain the authority and prerogatives which he had inherited from his ancestors, and claim to be the judge how far the innovations being inevitably wrought upon it by the labors of the missionaries should extend. It is needless to go into the details of this sad affair, and point out the last step in in the line of action pursued by the Prime Minister that led to the murder of the King; it is sufficient to state that a direct issue was made between the absolution of the King and the more liberal usages of the people of Western Europe, which issue was perhaps inevitable, and in which one party must meet with defeat, sealed and signalized by death. Yet we may mention one of the incidents in the contest which will serve to show the manner in which it was carried on. Formerly a certain form of respect had been paid to the idols when they were borne through the streets of the capital, and altogether unlike that which the Romanists exact for the host when it appears in public; and the King ordered similar demonstrations of respect, the lifting of hats, whenever the sick were carried through the streets. This was a kind of a compromise with Romanism and Paganism which the English decidely refused to comply with, and which of course served to hasten matters to their final issue. It was plain that one of the three conflicting powers must have the ascendency.

The King, though surrounded by his faithful detective police called the *Mena maso*, "red eyes," from the supposed continued strain to their eyes from difficult investigation, felt himself at last reduced to the necessity of legitimatizing murder in order to defend his authority from further encroachments. He announced his intention of issuing an order that any one who wished to fight with fire-arms, swords, or spears, might do so with impunity, even though death should result as a consequence. An order which, if carried out, would have placed all Europeans and Christians at the mercy of the idolaters of the island.

Under the direction of the Prime Minister the palace was surrounded by troops; several of the *Mena maso* were captured and killed, and the others demanded of the King. These he felt compelled to deliver up, though stipulating for their lives; and they were sent away to be ironed, as Christians had been under the reign of Ranavalona. The few troops with the King refused to fire upon those surrounding the palace, and the people, though pitying him, did not take up arms in his defence.

Soon after the death of the King, four of the chief nobles went to the Queen, with a written paper, which they handed to her, containing the conditions on which they proposed that the country should in future be governed. They requested her to read it, stating that if she consented to govern according to these conditions, they were willing that she should be the sovereign of the country, but that if she objected or declined, they must seek another ruler. The Queen, after reading the document, and listening to it, and receiving explanations on one or two points, expressed her entire and full consent to govern according to the plan therein set forth. The nobles then said, "We also bind ourselves by this agreement. If we break it, we shall be guilty of treason; and if you break it, we shall do as we have done now."

According to this document, the word of the sovereign alone was not to be law, but the nobles and heads of the people, together with the sovereign, were to make the laws.

Perfect liberty and protection were guaranteed to all foreigners who were obedient to the laws of the country.

Protection and liberty to worship, teach, and promote the extension of Christianity, were secured to the native Christians, and the same liberty and protection were guaranteed to those who were not Christians.

The wife of Radama II., who ascended the throne, was not a Christian, but while personally devoted to her idols and the sikidy, she remained true to her engagements. Instead of throwing obstacles in the way of the missionaries, she even encouraged attendance on religious worship and Christian instruction. She was of a mild and humane disposition, and the labors of the missionaries thrived under her administration. Ingenious reports were indeed spread abroad that the King was not dead, that he was still living, that his treaty with Mr. Lambert was valid, etc., well calculated to unsettle government and society, but order gradually became established, and the number of Christians increased to a degree that was almost astonishing. The Queen was in fact so lenient that it was suspected at times that she adhered to her idols merely as a matter of expediency, in order to retain a hold of the ancient prejudices of the country. The houses of worship were crowded every Sabbath.

Through the agency of military officers and traders the principles of the Christian religion became extended from the capital into the provinces; and every convert that was made among the natives, became a missionary, as it were, to his relatives and friends.

At length, in 1865, a treaty was ratified between the Government of Madagascar and Great Britain. In this treaty Earl

Russel, the English Minister, stipulated for provisions securing civil and religious freedom, both to native Christians and to missionaries. The Church has continued flourishing without interruption. In 1866 there were eight large congregations in the capital, which was then supposed to contain 30,000 inhabitants, and sixteen churches in the surrounding villages. It was estimated that in these villages there were 3,000 communicants and 15,000 converts; and there is every evidence that the Christian religion has taken a permanent hold of the people of Madagascar. In another generation it bids fair to be reckoned among the Christian nations of the earth.

From the year 1866 we do not meet with anything of much special interest concerning Madagascar until 1874, when two English gentlemen, Dr. Mullens and Mr. Pillan, visited the island to see what farther might be done there for extending the interests of the missionary cause. The result of this visit was, in the words of Dr. Mullens, "to shape out the framework of an enlarged mission." It was proposed to thoroughly fit up the training college for native pastors, to push forward the normal school system, and to make native agency more effective, and to encourage the missionaries by exciting a new interest in the work at home. There were about a thousand congregations organized in the island, though it was thought that the membership of sincere Christians was not over 30,000. The rolls did indeed contain 60,000 names, but in view of the facility and eagerness with which native pastors admitted members, it was believed that this number exaggerated the total of the true native Christians. But it was certain that the entire 300,000 among whom the Lon-London Society was laboring had renounced their idols and were in the way of becoming true converts to the Christian faith. The favorable report of these gentlemen doubtless stimulated the friends of the Society to renewed efforts. Besides the London Missionary Society, the Friends and Norwegians had promising missions on the island, each covering districts of about 100,000 people. In this year, 1874, an English Bishop was appointed for the island.

The next notice of the island that arrests our attention, and which needs to be recorded in order to give the reader an idea of the progress of the English missionary operations, is contained in the following statements of the special envoy of the British government, Gose Jones, to the Queen of Madagascar, in

1882. This gentleman stated at a public meeting in London that on landing at Tananarivo, whither he was sent as Commander-in-chief of the East Indian naval station to congratulate the Queen of Madagascar, he was surprised to find what manner of people the Malagasy were. He found Tananarivo to be a really splendid city, with magnificent public buildings. The house he lodged at was as good as any in London, and there was a Roman Catholic church which would not disgrace Paris.

The Prime Minister, who was, curiously enough, husband of the Queen, and almost the most intelligent, astute, and cleverest man he had ever met, occupied a splendid official residence.

The Premier knew precisely how far he could advance in the path of civilization, and where to stop. No outside people could so well control the Malagasy as the present Prime Minister. During the Queen's reign of ten years he had publicly abolished idol worship and embraced Christianity. The nobles of the land as well as the mass of the population were now Christians. The Premier was an educational reformer, and had established numerous schools. He had abolished "trial by poison," a superstitious rite which used to decimate the country. It was intended to make the Queen de facto as well as de jure the monarch of the island, and it was a great pity that any disturbance should come to the existing state of things. Among other beneficient changes the Prime Minister had wrought in the government of the island, at the hazard of his life, was the abolition of the introduction of slaves from Africa. He did this with one stroke of the pen, and in doing it he did away with what might be called the "material wealth" of Madagascar. A man had before been considered richer or poorer in proportion to the number of slaves he owned. A natural anxiety prevailed that a country which had so far progressed in civilization should not go back.

By the beginning of 1883 an embassy was received in England from the Queen of Madagascar, and its members were entertained by the government and people with the most respectful and considerate attention, everything of interest being shown to them in a way to heighten their regard for the Christian civilization and power of Great Britain, as well as for the kindness and benevolence of the citizens and missionaries.

This embassy subsequently visited the United States, where it arrived in the month of March 1883, and entered into treaty stipulations with our government. Thus, during the present century, and chiefly through missionary agency, Madagascar has passed from a state of pagan barbarism to one of Christian civilization, in which it has entered and taken a stand among the Christian nations of the world.

THE END.

www.ingramcontent.com/pod-product-compliance
Lightning Source LLC
Chambersburg PA
CBHW031445270326
41930CB00007B/869